Digital Militarism

Stanford Studies in Middle Eastern and Islamic Societies and Cultures

Digital Militarism

Israel's Occupation in the Social Media Age

Adi Kuntsman and Rebecca L. Stein

Stanford University Press

Stanford, California

Stanford University Press
Stanford, California

©2015 by the Board of Trustees of the Leland Stanford Junior University.
All rights reserved.

Printed in the United States of America on acid-free, archival-quality paper

Library of Congress Cataloging-in-Publication Data

Kuntsman, Adi, author.
  Digital militarism : Israel's occupation in the social media age / Adi Kuntsman
and Rebecca L. Stein.
      pages cm--(Stanford studies in Middle Eastern and Islamic societies and
cultures)
  Includes bibliographical references and index.
  ISBN 978-0-8047-8567-9 (cloth : alk. paper)--
  ISBN 978-0-8047-9490-9 (pbk. : alk. paper)
  1. Arab-Israeli conflict--Mass media and the conflict. 2. Israel-Arab War,
1967--Occupied territories. 3. Social media--Political aspects--Israel. 4. Digital
media--Political aspects--Israel. 5. Israel--Armed Forces--Gaza Strip. 6. Israel--
Armed Forces--West Bank. 7. Militarism--Israel. I. Stein, Rebecca L., author.
II. Title. III. Series: Stanford studies in Middle Eastern and Islamic societies and
cultures.
  DS119.76.K86 2015
  956.9405--dc23

                        2015001663

  ISBN 978-0-8047-9497-8 (electronic)

Typeset at Stanford University Press 11/13.5 Adobe Garamond Pro

To all those who are breaking the silence

Contents

Figures

Preface

WE BEGAN THIS BOOK in the midst of the Arab revolts of 2011. It was a time of political optimism. It was also a time of what some have called "cyber-utopianism."[1] As protestors with camera phones and Facebook accounts filled the streets of Tunisia and Egypt, many scholars and analysts hailed the political potential of social networking and mobile digital technologies as instruments of grassroots mobilizing, citizen empowerment, and democratic politics in the Middle East and beyond. In subsequent months and years, as pundits bemoaned the unraveling of the so-called Arab Spring, cyber-utopianism came under increasing criticism from scholars who stressed the politically variable nature of new digital information and communication technologies, including their utility in the hands of authoritarian regimes. But despite such correctives, and a wave of ensuing scholarship over the years that followed, much remained unexplored regarding the everyday ways that social networking could be tethered to repressive political projects, the ordinary means by which social media technologies and platforms could function as militarized tools in the hands of state and civilian users. This ordinariness is the focus of our book.

Digital Militarism is also a chronicle of Israel's military occupation of the Palestinian territories, read from the vantage of Israeli social media users and practices. More pointedly, it studies the everyday Israeli relationship to the occupation, with a focus on the role of social networking as agent and mediator within such relationships. What distinguishes our volume from the large literature on Israel's occupation is its attention to *both* the repressive state violence of which Israeli military rule is made and the myriad ways in which Israeli Jews support and sustain the state's violent regime through commonplace cultural practices, through acts of ordinary complicity.[2] Of course, ordinary complicity, in this context, is not new. But it takes a new shape in the digital age. Today, Israel's occupation regime is being bolstered by the routine social media practices of Jewish Israeli users—practices that pair the Israeli politics of militant nationalism with global networking conventions. *Digital Militarism* is a study of this interplay. It is also a portrait of growing Jewish Israeli political extremism of the past two decades and social media's increasing centrality within this political landscape.

When we began this book, the interplay between social media and militarist politics—the phenomenon we call *digital militarism*—was relatively anomalous in Israel, located largely on the Internet's margins, infrequently covered in the media, and poorly understood. Over the course of this book's development, the militarization of social media and other digital communication tools grew on a massive scale, commensurate with the global spread of social networking and mobile technologies themselves. Today, digital militarism is commonplace both in Israel and across global theaters. We have become accustomed to the Israeli military's deployment of social media as a public relations tool during incursions into the Gaza Strip; to real-time Twitter and Facebook updates from Israeli soldiers on patrol; to the presence of video-enabled smartphones at the scenes of violent confrontation between Israeli soldiers and Palestinians in the occupied territories. Such events now fail to surprise.

Because social media fields and practices are perpetually in flux, academic scholarship on this topic is always destined to suffer from a certain belatedness. Such was the case with this volume. Between the time of writing and publication, the popularity of particular networking platforms rose and fell, online practices shifted, global fads changed, as did the habits and norms of Israeli social media users. The problem of belatedness is also exacerbated by academic terminology. The very phrase "*new* media" seems to install a demand for contemporaneous criticism—documentation of the latest media trend, those practices unfolding *only now*—a demand that can obscure the histories of the media in question.[3] A different kind of belatedness attends scholarship on the Israeli military occupation. The pace of political developments on the ground—the rapid speed of settlement expansion, the serial Israeli incursions into the Gaza Strip—is so dizzying that timely political criticism is difficult if not elusive, particularly so in the medium of the book.

Given such inescapable belatedness, we propose an alternative reading strategy for those who engage with this book. Rather than approaching it through the lens of the current political and digital moment—a lens that invites the question "How current is this?"—we encourage a mode of reading that takes advantage of historical distance, with attention to what such distance makes uniquely visible in the material presented here. Framed in this light, what we hope will emerge from our book is something like an archive of Israeli occupation violence as rendered in social media forms; an archive of the everyday ways in which Israelis support and sustain state violence through digital means; an archive of digital complicity.

[handwritten marginalia: what they are creating ↓ an old archive]

We conclude this book in the immediate aftermath of Israel's bloody 2014 bombardment of the Gaza Strip, amidst Israeli state violence unleashed with almost unprecedented brutality against Palestinians living under occupation. Today, many commentators agree, the scale and degree of Jewish Israeli racism has never been higher. During the course of the incursion, as the Gazan death toll soared, we watched Jewish Israeli mobs hunt Palestinians in the street, chanting "Death to the Arabs." We watched as Israel's vanishingly small population of left-wing activists, those who do not support the state's military project in the occupied territories, were silenced, threatened, and attacked by their co-nationals. At this moment, Israel's occupation has never felt more entrenched.

In these difficult times, we turn to the archive of digital militarism as a possible source of political alternatives. The digital archive, as we envision it here, is not merely a body of documentation and a means of preservation. Rather, as we will propose in what follows, it is also a site from which the past might be opened for reconsideration. In the digital archive, acts of militarism and ordinary complicity are never over in any strict sense. Rather, they live on in digital form. And in the process, they are potentially available for a critical reopening, a hearing. In these militant times, even as the end to military occupation feels increasingly out of reach, we offer this archive with hopes for a future reckoning.

Digital Militarism

1

When Instagram Went to War
Israel's Occupation in the Social Media Age

"When you think *cyber*, think of Israel."

Israeli Prime Minister Netanyahu,
Cybertech 2014 Conference[1]

"Israelis are addicted to all forms of communicating and the very latest technology. Indeed, many of the world's instant messaging and communication systems were invented in Israel."

Israeli Ministry of Tourism,
promotional website[2]

"Israel is addicted to occupation."

Gideon Levy, 2014[3]

IN NOVEMBER 2012, during the Israeli aerial assault on the Gaza Strip of that year, many Israeli soldiers went into service with smartphones in their pockets, checking and updating their social media accounts from army installations as they awaited the start of the ground invasion.[4] The social networking field of the wartime moment was crowded and diverse, including users from a range of geographical locations and political standpoints. Official military spokespersons from Israel and Hamas joined thousands of civilian users from Israel, the Palestinian territories, and the international arena, anti-occupation activists numbering heavy among them, all of whom employed popular apps as political tools in what the global media called Israel's "first social media war."[5] The mobile uploads from individual soldiers differed markedly from the official output of the

Israeli military, with its emphasis on PR didacticism and the production of an institutional record. And they contrasted sharply with the viral content from Gaza's Palestinian residents that saturated global social networks, amateur documentation of the unfolding Israeli military devastation that was delivered to global users in the familiar staccato of digital real time. Israeli soldiers, for their part, chiefly employed social media to personalize the military campaign, to share images of mundane military scenes and army ephemera as they waited for the onset of the ground incursion (which would, in fact, never occur).

During these days of waiting, Israeli soldiers uploaded a series of selfies to their personal Instagram accounts.[6] In most respects, it was a standard catalogue of smartphone self-portraiture, including casual snapshots of uniformed young men and women smiling for the camera in compliance with Instagram's investment in the beauty of the ordinary, featuring everyday moments of military life in uniform: riding on a bus, posing for an elevator self-portrait, embracing a friend, all framed by the extended temporality of waiting, waiting to deploy (see Figures 1.1–1.4).[7] With the aid of retro filters, and their familiar aesthetics of the out of time and place, these mobile snapshots produced an exquisite and highly sanitized visual archive of soldiering. As such, they offered a digital twist on the long history of Israeli nationalist sentimentality and associated iconography, in which war is simultaneously heroized and aestheticized while disassociated from resultant violence.[8] Through the genre of the selfie, this iconography was mobilized to serve the needs of self-branding, with war configured as meme and employed as a tool of micro-celebrity.[9] These were images of militarism but not of battle, beautified bodies free of dirt or blood, at a considerable remove from the carnage of the concurrent military operation. The accompanying hashtag strings gestured toward the violence that the visual field had cleansed: #kill#sexy#nevergiveup#sleep#m16#instalove#happy and #war#army#soldier#artillery#fire#friends#cool#sad#israel#idf#instamood. Read together, the selfies and their hashtags generated unsettling intersections between the patriotic and the intimate, the lethal and the playful, the army and the algorithm.[10]

This book explores such intersections between social media and militarism: between ordinary networking practices and wartime violence, between the pleasure of commonplace digital acts and the brutality of Israel's

Continuance of the Status quo?

FIGURE 1.1. ISRAELI SOLDIER SELFIES I, INSTAGRAM, 2012. Israeli soldiers pose for selfies while awaiting their deployment for a ground invasion of the Gaza Strip. SOURCE: http://www.buzzfeed.com

FIGURE 1.2. ISRAELI SOLDIER SELFIES II, INSTAGRAM, 2012.
SOURCE: http://www.buzzfeed.com

FIGURE 1.3. ISRAELI SOLDIER SELFIES III, INSTAGRAM, 2012.
SOURCE: http://www.buzzfeed.com

FIGURE 1.4. ISRAELI SOLDIER SELFIES IV, INSTAGRAM, 2012.
SOURCE: http://www.buzzfeed.com

military occupation.[11] We term this phenomenon *digital militarism*. In our rendering, *digital militarism* describes the process by which digital communication platforms and consumer practices have, over the course of the first two decades of the twenty-first century, become militarized tools in the hands of state and nonstate actors, both in the field of military operations and in civilian frameworks. In the broadest terms, the *digital* of digital militarism is a highly varied domain of new technologies and technological aptitudes, including high-tech weaponry and cyberwarfare—a field in which the Israeli military proudly excels. Our investigation focuses chiefly on the role of social media and enabling mobile technologies within this framework, with attention to how they have been mobilized by Israeli state and civilian "networked publics" as tools, sites, and languages of militarist engagement.[12] Hence, we use *digital militarism* to refer to the extension of militarized culture into social media domains often deemed beyond the reach of state violence, and to the impact of militarization on everyday Israeli social networking. We are proposing, then, that both terms in this equation shape the other: namely, that the evolving terms of social media usage impact the field of Israeli militarism, just as shifts in Israeli militarization are altering the social media field. Digital militarism allows us to think beyond the paradigm of the repressive Israeli military state in an effort to make visible the varied and often ordinary ways in which Israel's military regime and pervasive culture of militarism are perpetuated and sustained.

The militarization of social media is by no means unique to the Israeli context. Rather, as is by now something of a truism, social media have been integrated into military operations in contexts across the globe, with platforms such as Twitter, Instagram, and YouTube employed for wartime PR, as tools of surveillance and counter-insurgency, and as archives of perpetrator violence. In the social media age, contemporary warfare and armed conflicts have increasingly encompassed digital communication platforms—a process that has enlarged theaters of military operation and changed our understanding of the political function and political ends of digital technologies.[13] In recent years we have seen the increasing incorporation of social media into the military toolboxes of Western states, employed to win hearts and minds and conduct counter-terrorism. Today, violent conflicts between states, or with stateless groups, take shape on social networks—digital battlefields deemed vital to the success of conventional military operations on the ground. Today, we expect the presence of smartphones, computers, and video-enabled cameras on the battlefield; the integration of social networking into military arsenals; the real-time Twitter and Facebook updates from war zones; the violent footage filmed and shared by the perpetrators themselves. Digital militarism was once an aberration, located on the periphery of the Internet and its associated social worlds. By 2014, it had become commonplace.[14]

Although digital militarism has diverse geopolitical coordinates, this book studies the ways it takes shape in the contemporary Israeli context and the history of its emergence.[15] We argue that within a global culture of mobile capture and viral circulation, Israeli militarism is being reframed and recruited by ordinary Israeli users and their international supporters as part of the social media everyday. In Israel today, mainstream militarized politics are being interwoven with global networking protocols: their grammars, aesthetic norms, structures of feeling, and modes of consumer engagement. On platforms such as Facebook and Instagram, the classic terms and aesthetics of Zionist settler-nationalism are being reshaped in compliance with networking norms. Like any global phenomenon, this interplay between militarism and social media necessarily takes highly localized forms, a process by which global protocols are retooled to articulate national needs. It is precisely this process of localization that concerns us here.

While broader histories of Israeli militarism inform this book, we focus on how digital militarism functions in the context of Israel's ongoing military occupation of the Palestinian territories. In particular, we are interested in the ways that social networking practices are mediating the everyday Israeli relationship to military rule. Our objects of analysis, then, include the Israeli soldier in the occupied West Bank or Gaza Strip with a smartphone in his or her pocket for whom routine army operations have been rebranded as a potential "share." They include official *ethical infractions* Israeli military bodies endeavoring to incorporate social media into the state's toolbox. And they include ordinary Jewish Israeli civilians and pro-Israeli supporters outside the nation-state who consume and circulate digital images of Israel's occupation from the comfort of their mobile devices, often while the military operation is unfolding. In all of these instances, ordinary social media practices and users are being conscripted into the state's military project. And in the process, state violence is being practiced through other means—through acts of "liking" and "sharing," through the visual syntax of the selfie, through the structures of feeling that social networking make uniquely possible.[16]

A central tension lies at the core of digital militarism: namely, the ways it renders the Israeli occupation at once palpable and out of reach, both visible and invisible. On the one hand, mobile technologies have made the spectacle of state violence instantly available, often in real time, in the palm of the hand on smartphone screens. As such, digital militarism has the potential to extend Israel's occupation into the most private Israeli spaces and times, the most mundane networking contexts, zones of Internet activity typically deemed beyond the purview of Israel's military projects. At the same time, the patina of the digital everyday can minimize and banalize this violence, obscuring its visibility and mitigating its impact. Such tensions undergird this study.

The Innovation Nation and Its Vanishing Occupation

Our analysis concentrates on a particular historical period of Israeli digital militarism: 2008–2014, the years of its development, consolidation, and eventual normalization. These were years of growing social media literacy in political arenas across the globe, years in which mobile digital technologies were becoming more affordable and more pervasive. During this short span of time, digital militarism moved from the margins of Israeli society to its center. Initially, the interplay between social networking and militarized projects of various kinds took Israelis by surprise, alternately lauded by the Israeli media in the language of digital pioneering (as when the Israeli military began to experiment with networking tools) or condemned by pundits as scandalous aberrations (as when the private Facebook posts of soldiers, depicting military abuse, became widely exposed). By the end of the period in question, militarism had been fully incorporated into Israeli digital culture.

Israelis have long been celebrated for their technological literacy and have long enjoyed high per-capita penetration of information and communication technologies.[17] During these years, this literacy was extending to new digital communication tools, aesthetics, and grammar. In 2011,

Israel was deemed one of "the world's biggest users of social networks."[18] In 2014, Israelis were said to spend the most per-capita time engaged in social networking, celebrated as a global leader in digital technology adoption.[19] At the same time, Israel's much-touted high-tech sector continued its growth as an international leader in technological innovation, representing what some have called the most important technology incubator next to Silicon Valley—its growth fueled by the sector's close ties to the military industrial complex, with technologies honed in militarized contexts frequently reengineered for civilian ones.[20] It was during these years that Israel was famously dubbed the "Start Up Nation" and later the "innovation nation," a branded concept installed to retell a classic Zionist modernizing narrative, a formulation that some have termed "High-Tech Zionism."[21] For the state's "Brand Israel" campaign, the discourse of technological innovation could be effectively mobilized to supplant the deleterious global story of military occupation and conflict. Technology, in this rendering, functioned as the occupation's surrogate.

The growth of the Israeli high-tech economy, and the spread of social media within the Israeli populace, was coterminous with a very particular chapter in the history of the military occupation and Israeli militarism more generally. In the mid-to-late 2000s, while Israelis were learning the art of social media, mainstream Israeli political agendas were changing. In prior decades, the so-called "Arab-Israeli conflict" (or, euphemistically, the "situation," *hamatzav* [in Hebrew]) had dominated the national political agenda.[22] But in these years, the perceived importance of the conflict began to wane, as mainstream Jewish Israeli society began to lose interest in the "peace process" and matters of occupation.[23] Such disinterest was enabled by the strong Israeli economy of this period, and the spatial fiction advanced by the separation barrier—a structure that enabled Israelis to live *as if* at a remove from Palestinians under occupation.[24] It was also bolstered by Israel's unilateral withdrawal or "disengagement" from the Gaza Strip in 2005, a political euphemism that obscured the continuation of military occupation over the Gaza Strip, albeit in new forms.[25] In the years following disengagement, many Jewish Israelis would insist that "there is no occupation in Gaza," the language of "war" replacing and obfuscating that of "military occupation" during Israel's successive incursions into the Gaza Strip (2008–2009, 2012, 2014).

Gaza: Still under military occupation

As Jewish Israelis turned away from the military occupation, domestic issues began to figure more centrally in the national political agenda, chiefly matters of economy and "lifestyle" that had been thought to exist at a remove from matters of military rule (a formula that framed the mass Israeli social protests of 2011).[26] The national elections of 2012, for their part, were conducted in the absence of a robust public discussion about Israel's relationship with the Palestinians. In the same year, a judiciary panel convened by Israeli Prime Minister Netanyahu would "reject the claim that Israel's presence in the territory is that of an occupying force," an opinion that aimed to pave the way for widespread settlement in the West Bank.[27] In the Israeli media, images and discussion of Israel's military rule were receding, relegated to the domain of "non-news" (in the words of one Israeli blogger).[28] In broader political discourse, Palestinians rarely appeared, save in the language of "terrorism" and "security threat." In some centrist and right-wing discourse, Israeli pundits went further by disavowing Israel's occupation altogether, referring to the term only in quotation marks.[29]

And yet, Israeli military rule in the Palestinian territories continued and flourished during these years, as did the Jewish settlement population in the West Bank, supported by an ever-expanding road network.[30] And even as the occupation was receding from political discourse, Jewish Israelis were progressively embracing a politics of militant patriotism. Racist anti-Palestinian sentiment once relegated to Israeli right-wing margins moved to the center of mainstream political discourse, the evolution of a set of rightward shifts that began in 2000, growing in force and magnitude during the periodic military assaults on Gaza.[31] During such operations, many Jewish Israelis would support a politics of militant security in the name of "Israel's right to self-defense," usually with little regard for mounting Palestinian civilian casualties. The chorus of militancy would grow markedly during Israel's 2014 Gaza offensive. As the Palestinian death toll from Israeli military actions grew, enabled by widespread popular Israeli support for the operation, left-wing pundits spoke with new candor about the Israeli "culture of hate[. . .]and vengeance," about "an environment where casual racism is a norm."[32] The Israeli public of the wartime period had little patience for a discussion of Palestinian dead and wounded. Even recitation of their names was considered a slanderous act. The Israeli appetite for militancy, on the other hand, had never been stronger.

Our discussion of digital militarism focuses on the intersection of these historical and social processes: increasing digital literacy among Jewish Israeli populations and an Israeli political landscape characterized by growing patriotic militarism and denial of occupation. These coterminous developments are typically viewed as separate phenomena. Instead, we suggest that they are mutually productive, that they function together and through each other.

Israeli Militarism and the Everyday

Over the course of the past two decades, an extensive literature has emerged on the political function of new communication technologies in varied geopolitical contexts. While drawing on this literature, we hope to temper its recalcitrant investment in the counter-hegemonic potential of social media as a political force, an investment enlivened by the Arab revolts of 2011 and often framed by the language of "digital democracy" or "liberation technology."[33] In the wake of these revolts, as we noted in our Preface, many commentators placed credit at the feet of social networking, some proposing that Facebook and Twitter, and the mobile technologies that enable them, were naturally suited to the political projects of insurgent social movements.[34] It was only later that scholars began to consider the politically variable nature of these new technologies, including the ways they have been employed by dictators and police states as public relations platforms, as tools for tracking and monitoring political dissidents, and as means of counter-insurgency more generally.[35] A critique of the enduring "liberation technology" paradigm frames our analysis throughout.

Digital Militarism also draws on earlier scholarship on cyberwars and cyberconflict, on the use of digital media for information warfare and more direct modes of computer-based combat such as hacking attacks on computer infrastructures and databases.[36] The cyberconflict literature aimed to account for the displacement of violence into the domain of the Internet, a process by which war and conflict were articulated through the language of the technical, and by which the technical itself became militarized. But often missing from this scholarship was a textured sense of the ordinary social processes on which techno-militarism depends— that is, the *everydayness* of militarized projects, their absorption into the most banal of normal civilian acts, or what might be termed the unbearable lightness of digital militarism.

In attending to this gap, we draw on a voluminous scholarship on Israeli militarism and its relationship to the civilian everyday.[37] As this scholarship makes evident, Israeli militarism's presence in Israeli civilian life can be traced to the very beginnings of Zionist settler-nationalist projects—a presence that far exceeds the military base, the battlefield, or the broader field of military operations. This scholarship has been attentive to militarism's impact on popular film, literature, and music; on educational policy and pedagogy; on children's play and fantasies; on the intimate and personal domains of family and body, gender relations, and sexual practices; and on the ways that quotidian consumer practices and institutions have been increasingly drawn into Israel's security cartography.[38] Baruch Kimmerling, the foremost theorist of Israeli militarism, famously described this phenomenon as Israeli "civil militarism" and "militarism of the mind,"[39] concepts that aimed to illustrate the nation's perpetual orientation toward war preparation, its reigning discourses of security threat and regional enmity, and the penetration of military mores into the most mundane and private civilian domains.[40]

Following Kimmerling and other scholars of Israeli militarism, we argue that militarism also takes shape in the realm of social media—in everyday networking practices, visual protocols and grammars, and digitized "ordinary affects."[41] But if Kimmerling's notion of civil militarism stressed the expansion of militarist logic from the battlefield into civilian life, we propose that the workings and effects of digital militarism are not unidirectional. Rather, militarism has shaped social media culture, even as ordinary social media practices have remade the sphere of militarism itself. While Israeli militarism has long been embedded in everyday civilian life, digital militarism, we propose, has changed the terms of this relationship.

Militarized Hashtags and Digital Times

How, precisely, do spheres of militarism and digital culture inflect and produce each other? To briefly consider this question, we return to the wartime selfies with which we began. Circulated widely and popularly, they achieved almost instantaneous virality, both in Israel and internationally. Some users responded with disgust to these aestheticized self-portraits of wartime waiting.[42] Others defended the photographers and their subjects, insisting that they were merely young people trying to live their normal lives (a standard national narrative that casts soldiers as victims). Still others called them surreal and wholly unexpected as a photographic archive of a nation at war.

What startled about this visual archive was the stark interplay between violence and its absence. On the one hand, these photographs reinstalled a familiar Israeli iconography of militarism, casting soldiers as beautiful and often erotic subjects. Their captions, too, spoke in the conventional language of militant patriotism: "We're coming for you, Gaza," "Out in the sun, in the dust of the war, one nation standing stronger than before," "Ready to defend my country." In the process, they articulated a set of familiar Israeli wartime dreams: killing in the name of national security, eradicating enemies and returning unharmed. Yet the visual language of the selfie interrupted the wartime storyline. For despite army uniforms and weapons, these mobile self-portraits powerfully articulated the banality of the *not war* through strict adherence to selfie conventions, replete with "duckface" for the camera, hand gestures, and the iconic elevator mirror. The hashtags, for their part, offered a messier picture in which violence (#5.56, #bomb) coexisted with everyday networking pleasures (#instagood, #happy). Read as a field of digital poetics rather than a mere algorithmic instrument, they articulated a central tenet of digital militarism: the conjunction of militarized dispositions and social media commonplace.[43] *uncommonplace coexisting w/ commonplace*

The complexity of this photographic archive also rests in its polyvalent temporality. Read as a body of selfies, the archive traffics in the time of *the now*, in the perpetual present tense. This is the foremost time of global *lines blurred* social media, installed through the live-feed, the presumed instantaneity of the viral circuit, the immediacy of Facebook and Twitter updates. Yet the images also speak in the ambivalent time of the *yet to come*, evident in scenes of collective waiting for an impending ground invasion, a field of suspended time in which military engagement exists in the modality of an imprecise but certain future. Where most Israelis are concerned, the future war has always already been foretold and secured, its violence obviated through inevitability, even if its coordinates cannot be anticipated.

instantaneity of pasts coexist w/ anticipation of war

Through Instagram's retro-filter, this futurity takes the paradoxical form of nostalgia, a haunted future already played out in the past, already anticipated by a history of past wars.[44] In that sense, the time of the *not yet war* collapses into the normalized national time of the *always war*, evident in perpetual Israeli preparation for the next war, even before the current military campaign has drawn to a close.[45]

These intertwined temporalities index the conflictual time of Israeli digital militarism more broadly. This field is at once embedded in the global social media world with its immediacy, its viral circulation, its real time. But it is also rooted in the long history of Zionist settler-nationalism and its mythology of perpetual war. Digital militarism spans these historical and temporal divides, speaking through both registers, bringing Israeli military histories and social media times into intimate articulation.

Viral Fictions, Ordinary Archives

We have argued that a series of contrasts and tensions undergird the field of Israeli digital militarism. They are evident in the relationship between violence and not-violence, between killing and eroticism, war and self-branding, security emergencies and everyday moments. They cohere in the spatial interplay between Jewish Israeli users of mobile technologies at home and soldiers on a military base waiting to deploy. They emerge in the temporal contrasts between Israeli militarism in real time and Israeli militarism with its long history, between the *not yet* (*war*) and the *always* (*war*). They take shape in coterminus historical developments: growing social media literacy in Israel and declining political interest in Israel's military occupation. And they appear in the tension between the fiction of a vanishing occupation and the occupation's ongoing consolidation on the ground—a consolidation evident in soldiers' status updates, Instagram selfies shot on patrol, and militarized Twitter feeds.

Lying dormant in these contrasts is a military occupation that is both absent and ever-present, both missing from view and spectacularly visible. This impossible rift lies at digital militarism's core: a tension between virality and obfuscation, exposure and concealment, the spectacular visibility of Israel's repressive military rule and the increasing Israeli refusal to acknowledge it as such. Such a tension is best understood as what anthropologist Michael Taussig has called a "public secret"—namely, a secret that is known to the public but which the public chooses to keep from itself though various cultural strategies and mechanisms, something that is known but cannot be articulated within the terms of governing social norms.[46] According to Taussig, the public secret is about "knowing what not to know," about living with one's complicity with violence, about participating in and sustaining social institutions of racism, incarceration, and even slavery. In the Israeli context, this notion of public secrecy aims to account for the normative Israeli fantasy of a missing occupation, for modes of Israeli living in a state of perpetual *as if*: as if the Israeli state violence in the West Bank and Gaza Strip did not spill into everyday life in Jewish Israeli cities, as if Israeli democracy was not undercut by its concurrent military rule, as if these regimes (democracy and military rule) "were not one."[47] The public secret is a form of social contract that works to contain the effects of Israeli state violence on the civilian everyday.[48]

Of course, the Israeli public secret is not unique to the digital age. In some respects, it can be traced to the very founding of the Zionist settlement project and the colonial fictions on which it relied (a "land without a people for a people without a land"). By extension, one finds its roots in state policy and Israeli discourse about the Palestinian dispossession of 1948—namely, the collective Israeli refusal to contend with histories of Palestinian expulsion at Israeli hands. Nor is the Israeli public secret a static form. For the object of secrecy, that which is not known by the Israeli mainstream, vacillates in accordance with the changing terms of the Israeli political landscape. At certain moments and in certain contexts, then, the object of secrecy can come back into visibility, and sometimes with very unsettling social effects.[49] Israeli strategies of secrecy preservation are equally dynamic—changing with the political landscape. We argue that public secrecy has taken new forms in the social media age. Today, social media and social networking function as crucial sites and tools of secrecy management. They have provided a new field of practices, a new body of grammars and visual syntax by which Israelis can sustain the public secret within the framework of the digital everyday.

✓ and anonymity

Our journey through Israeli digital militarism begins historically, with a study of its growth in the first two decades of the twenty-first century. In Chapter 2, we examine the ways that social media have been incorporated into the toolbox of the Israeli state during times of war and military incursion in its occupied territories. We are particularly attentive to the military's adoption of personalized social networking as a means of effective statecraft by which state violence is remade as everyday digital play. Chapter 3 studies a landmark case in the history of digital militarism: the 2010 Facebook album of former Israeli soldier Eden Abergil, whose snapshots with bound and blindfolded Palestinian detainees, uploaded to her Facebook account, generated an Israeli scandal. Here we study the varying strategies employed by Israeli publics to manage the event's dangerous virality—chiefly, the ways that public discussion of the scandal turned away from military occupation onto questions of social media themselves. Chapter 4 considers how Israelis have used the charge of "digital doctoring" to forestall public discussion of Israeli state violence—namely, by mounting the charge that images of Palestinian deaths are produced for political effect. Through this discourse, particularly rampant during military incursions into Gaza, discussion of Israeli state violence is replaced with concerns about digital authenticity—a political formation we term "digital suspicion." Chapter 5 and the Afterword reflect on the gradual normalization of Israeli digital militarism during years studied in this volume (2008–2014). We focus on the growth of what we term "selfie militarism," a genre that circulated heavily during and prior to the 2014 Israeli military offensive into the Gaza Strip. The viral spread of the militarized selfie, we argue, indexes the normalization of both digital militarism and the military occupation itself.

Taken together, the chapters that follow consider key episodes in the history of Israeli digital militarism. Many are framed by Israel's successive military incursions into the Gaza Strip (2008–2009, 2012, 2014) and the Israeli social media fields that accompanied them. Such incursions were crucial in the development and evolution of digital militarism. In their midst, the military's social media policy would be practiced and honed, while Israeli networked publics would mobilize online in large numbers to support their state, cultivating the terms of their militarized engagement. Our analysis focuses heavily on *viral* events in the history of digital militarism—events that were spectacularly visible on Israeli social networks, heavily consumed and debated by Israeli and pro-Israeli international users. But in our reading, their virality often worked to obfuscate rather than to expose the workings of Israeli militarism and public secrecy. And perhaps counterintuitively, the media narratives that tracked these events often reproduced the invisibility of the military occupation, their virality working to bolster rather than destabilize the public secret. In what follows, we reread these episodes with attention to that which their virality obscured. In the course of such episodes, Israeli militarism was remaking the sphere of social networking and digital communications, even as social networking practices and protocols were refiguring the terms of Israeli militarism. This mutually productive encounter—one which continues to unfold in the Israeli present—is the subject of this book.

2

"Another War Zone"
The Development of Digital Militarism

"The blogosphere and the new media are another war zone. We have to be relevant here."

IDF Spokesperson, 2008[1]

"Computers and keyboards are the weapons, Facebook and Twitter are the battlefields. It is there that we fight, each and every day."

IDF Spokesperson,
New Media Division, 2011[2]

"We all share a responsibility to explain our fight to the world."

The Truth About the Middle East,
Israeli Facebook group, 2012[3]

"We are [operating] on four fronts: The military front, the home front, the diplomatic front and the public diplomacy front. We must fight for the truth, for the facts, and your help is worth more than gold . . . refuting the industry of lies."

Prime Minster Netanyahu,
praising Israeli social media volunteers, 2014[4]

WHEN ISRAEL LAUNCHED its aerial assault on the Gaza Strip on November 14, 2012, citing mounting Hamas rocket fire on Israeli territory as its rationale, neither Israeli nor international observers were wholly surprised. For however devastating the results on Palestinian lives and infrastructures, such operations had already been assimilated into the state's military occupation policy, operations so normalized as to mer-it the chilling military euphemism "mowing the lawn."[5] But what did take these observers by surprise was the campaign's extension into social media from the early hours of its onset, not merely by civilian users in multiple locales (Israel, Palestine, and the international arena) but by the Israeli military's official social media unit. The military selected its dedicated Twitter feed to announce the operation's onset while they also prepared content on other platforms (such as YouTube, Flickr, Pinterest, and Facebook).[6] The IDF's second tweet broadcast the assassination of Hamas military commander Ahmad al-Ja'bari, with a colorized image of his face posted to their Facebook page shortly thereafter, its composition and cherry-red filter more befitting a movie poster or gaming interface, some bloggers mused, than wartime public relations (Figure 2.1).[7] Hamas responded in kind, employing its own Twitter feed to warn advancing Israeli soldiers of their impending demise (Figure 2.2).[8]

By the end of the military campaign's second day, the notion of a "Twitter War" or "Social Media Battlefield" had become a journalis-tic cliché as numerous online commentators mulled this unexpectedly trendy shift in Israeli military strategy. Many pundits spoke in the lan-guage of novelty, lauding "the first Twitter declaration of war," the first "military operation live-blogged in real time," and "the first social media war between Israel and Hamas."[9] Some asked, Was Israel charting new modes of warcraft? Would future wars in other geopolitical contexts be molded in Israel's likeness, employing a toolbox comprising Twitter, Facebook, YouTube, and Flickr?[10] Such questions scarcely masked a sense of technophilic wonder, as if once again, and even under rocket fire, Is-raeli modernity had triumphed.

This fascination with technological novelty is unique neither to this geopolitical case nor to this historical moment. A discourse of newness, typically linked to a claim for utopian transformation, has attended the emergence of many technologies, of which digital communication tech-nologies are but the latest.[11] One saw a version of this discourse emerge in the immediate aftermath of the 2011 Arab revolts, taking shape in utopian claims about the ways that social media were making grassroots mobilization possible in hitherto unavailable ways. In keeping with the temporal idiom of "the first time," this narrative told a story of revolutions

Ahmed Jabari: Eliminated.

pic.twitter.com/sCnQnKkM

← Reply   ⟲ Retweet   ★ Favorite

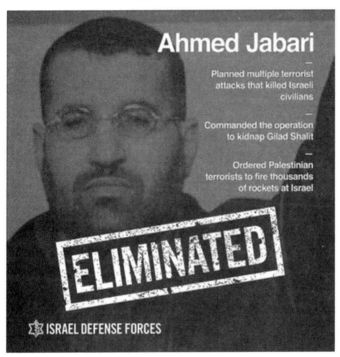

626	163
RETWEETS	FAVORITES

9:21 PM - 14 Nov 12 · Embed this Tweet   Flag media

FIGURE 2.1. MILITARY CINEMATICS, #IDFSPOKESMAN, TWITTER, 2012. Israeli
military announces their assassination of Hamas military commander Ahmad
al-Jaʿbari, 14 November 2012. SOURCE: https://twitter.com/idfspokesperson

FIGURE 2.2. TWITTER WARS, TWITTER, 2012. Exchange between #IDFSpokesman and #AlQassamBrigade (Hamas). SOURCE: https://twitter.com/

that were *only now* possible through the aid of these technologies, a fiction that installed social media as the chief agent of populist political change (technological determinism at work). Among scholars, the lure of such claims may rest in the tautological effect of academic jargon—"new media" instantiate newness—a tautology harnessed to explain moments of historic rupture.[12] This apparent truism is abetted by the discourse of technological innovation with its fetishization of progress and companion notion of rapid technological obsolescence. As corrective, some historians of technology have usefully reminded us that "all media were once new"—a statement whose simplicity belies the extent of our investment in novelty claims where digital technologies are concerned.[13]

The narrative of a "first social media war" partook of this discourse, replete with its constitutive blind spots, chiefly its failure to attend to history. In the Israeli case, the first-time story concealed both the longer history of Internet and social media militarization in the Israel context and the longer history of Israeli occupation violence, of which the Gaza attacks were but the latest installment. This chapter tracks digital militarism's gradual development from 2000 to 2012—a response, in part, to the amnesic nature of the first-time narrative. And herein lies a tension. For our critique of this narrative notwithstanding, we argue that a substantial shift in the domain of Israeli digital militarism was indeed at work during this period, in varying ways and degrees. These were pivotal years in the development of digital militarism—years in which Israeli social media users would be conscripted in large numbers, and in which the central conventions governing this digital playing field were being consolidated. What began as hacker subculture among a small group of computer-savvy Israeli youths would, within a two-decade period, massively expand in scale, being eventually incorporated into Israeli military PR policy, particularly during times of war. In the course of this expansion, everyday Israeli social media users would gradually become conscripts, both willing and otherwise, within the state's occupation project.

A full compendium of recent developments in the field of militarized social media is beyond the scope of this chapter.[14] Rather, we focus on developments in the field of digital militarism that accompanied the central Israeli military campaigns of the first two decades of the twenty-first century: namely, Israel's 2006 aerial and naval bombardment of Lebanon and its 2008–2009 and 2012 military incursions into the Gaza Strip.[15] In their midst and aftermath the military's social media policy would be honed and elaborated, while networked Israeli publics would mobilize in large numbers to support their state, cultivating the terms and grammar of their militarized engagement. We are proposing that the growth of militarized social networking was both product and progenitor of such episodes of organized state violence. In the process, the terms of state violence were being transformed.

Cyberwarfare: Digital Militarism's Early Days

In Israel, as in many other geopolitical contexts, the militarization of the Internet began in the form of hacking. In September of 2000, a small cadre of tech-savvy Israeli youths hacked the websites of Hamas and Hizballah, the Lebanese Shi'i movement whose militia have been fighting the Israeli security forces in southern Lebanon.[16] Their strategy centered on denial of service (DoS) attacks and website defacements, replacing existing content with Israeli national symbols or slogans, political taunts, and occasional pornography.[17] Hizballah's homepage was among those targeted, its content supplanted with an Israeli flag and a music file playing the Israeli national anthem. The timing was highly calculated, spurred by the failure of talks at Camp David, the outbreak of the second Palestinian Intifada, and Hizballah's abduction of three Israeli soldiers—all occurring within the preceding year. And Palestinian hackers would retaliate promptly, attacking the websites of the Israeli Defense Forces, the Israeli Parliament,[18] and Israeli and American financial institutions and sites of e-commerce, the latter adversely affecting the Israeli stock market.[19] The Israeli CEO of the Internet provider NetVision described the unfolding events as "the first full-scale war in cyberspace."[20]

These were not isolated events. In November of the same year, anti-Israeli hackers attacked the American-Israeli Public Affairs Committee (AIPAC), publishing emails from AIPAC databases and credit card numbers of its members to "protest the atrocities in Palestine."[21] In return, a pro-Israeli hacker posted the mobile phone numbers of Palestinian leaders as well as details of the chief websites and IRC servers through which the Palestinian movement communicated.[22] In 2001, a group of Israeli hackers named "mosad" defaced the website of Al-Manar television, the official channel of Hizballah. In the same year, pro-Israeli hackers shut down the website of the official Palestinian news agency, Wafa, and replaced an unofficial Hamas site with a pornographic link. During Israel's 2002 reoccupation of the West Bank, which resulted in the destruction of a large number of Palestinian ISPs, switchboards, and TV and radio stations, civilian cyberwarfare among pro-Israeli and pro-Palestinian supporters on the Internet attempted to support conventional military tactics on the ground.[23] In contrast to hacking attacks in other geopolitical contexts, "a game controlled by a few highly specialized" individuals, these episodes included thousands of Israelis and pro-Israelis who engaged in cyberbattle with their young counterparts in Palestine and the broader Arab world, their actions enabled by detailed online instructions for cyberbattle.[24] Together, these actors were refashioning regional politics in the technical terms of competing hacker abilities.[25]

Cyberwarfare of this kind intensified during the 2006 war between Israel and the Lebanese Shi'i movement Hizballah. Indeed, that war represented the first instance in the history of the Arab-Israeli conflict in which virtual and real battle spaces were actively conjoined. In addition to hacking, new web technologies were enlisted in the waging of psychological warfare. Israeli hackers used Google Earth to identify areas where the Israeli army had successfully targeted Hizballah's positions, while Hizballah employed the same service to identify Israeli-wrought destruction in civilian areas.[26] As Hizballah hacked Israeli state websites, the Israeli military hacked the Al-Manar TV channel and acquired control of Hizballah radio airways, retooling them as platforms for Israeli propaganda.[27] *hacking media sources to flip them to the other side*

These episodes drew media and popular attention to the emerging digital terrain of the broader Arab-Israeli conflict. For some Israelis, cyberwarfare raised concerns about terror's new frontier,[28] while others warned about new security breaches.[29] For the Israeli state, these incidents also invited a strategic reconsideration of official policy. In the aftermath of the 2006 war, critics argued that the Israeli state had grossly neglected to take cyberspace seriously by focusing chiefly on traditional modes of information dissemination and psychological warfare (for example, dropping leaflets, jamming broadcasts, and so on).[30] Indeed, many credited Hizballah with a public relations victory in superior use of cyberspace to deliver its political message.[31]

These early years were crucial precursors of today's digital militarism. The hacking attacks of the early-to-mid 2000s represented the first instance in the history of the Arab-Israeli conflict in which military warfare and civilian use of new communication technologies had been actively conjoined—a process in which digital communications had been remade as a new body of targets, weapons, and battlefields in their own right. And these years evidenced the growing engagement of Israeli civilians in the field of digital warfare. The Jewish Israeli public had long been militarized; this, in itself, was not new. But now they were conscripting communication technologies into the process, wielding them as battlefield

role of Israeli citizens in field of digital warfare → Jewish-Israeli public = militarized

instruments—placing Internet communication and digital creativity into patriotic service. This process transformed the terms of Israeli militarism and created new relations between civilians and soldiers, between home and battlefield, between acts of wit and acts of violence. All would pave the way for forms of digital militarism to come.

Cast Lead: Conscripting Social Media

Gaza incursion

Israeli online communities first became militarized on a massive scale during the 2008–2009 military incursion in the Gaza Strip, code-named "Operation Cast Lead."[32] During the course of the operation, unprecedented numbers of Israeli civilians employed the Internet and social media platforms to debate the unfolding events. Hebrew-language news websites were overwhelmed by comments from loyal citizens, often directing vitriol against the Israeli left. Many Israelis engaged in global digital dialogues in an attempt to defend the country's image. The U.S.-based Israel advocacy group "Stand With US" recruited Israeli and international volunteers to support the state in online forums. Many thousands joined their Israel "command center."[33] While Israeli leftists and anti-occupation activists were also active on social media platforms, the voices of militant Israeli patriots dominated during the incursion in accordance with the widespread Jewish Israeli support for the military's actions.[34]

Although much of this patriotic networked engagement took place in Hebrew or English, other Israeli linguistic communities were also involved. A telling example was the Russian-Israeli blogosphere, consisting primarily of recent immigrants from the former Soviet Union, their online engagement concentrated in the Russian-language blogging network LiveJournal.[35] Here, users worked tirelessly to defend their new country, support the Israeli military project, and combat "pro-Palestinian media bias."[36] "The world does not see, does not understand an ORDINARY Israeli. It does understand an ARAB who is screaming and crying hysterically, every day on television screens. But we are modest, and our voice is not heard," wrote a leader of one such blogging community.[37] Militantly patriotic and often explicitly right wing, they aimed to speak for all of Israel rather than merely its immigrant population.[38] These bloggers favored personalized narratives to make their case, using private experiences and ordinary voices to express patriotism, a precursor to the kinds of personalized militarism that would proliferate on Hebrew-language social networks in subsequent years.

The 2008–2009 Gaza incursion was a landmark: the Israeli military's first official use of social media. The need for social media PR emerged from the lessons of the second Lebanon war with Hizballah (2006), in which the Israeli military was said to have lost the information battle due to numerous technological missteps.[39] As a corrective, social media were conscripted by the military as PR tools from the onset of the 2008–2009 operations. It was a highly improvisational effort, involving considerable trial and error and complementing the state's ban on the entry of foreign and Israeli journalists into Gaza, in an attempt to manage the wartime message.[40] On December 29, 2008, with the incursion still in its early days, the IDF launched a dedicated YouTube channel—the first social media platform with which the military would experiment. Employing English and aimed chiefly at an international audience, it presented black and white aerial footage of Israeli military attacks and video blogs from IDF spokespersons that aimed to justify the course of the ongoing operation.[41] The most popular videos involved aerial footage taken from the vantage of the weapon, targets circled in color and augmented with descriptive notes (for example, "Although the site appears to be empty, secondary explosion confirms presence of concealed rockets").[42] As with prior military use of aerial footage, both in this and other geopolitical contexts, these videos endeavored to justify and sterilize the air campaign through a visual logic that rendered all persons and buildings seen from above as proto-targets (Figure 2.3).[43] The YouTube channel boasted more than four thousand subscribers in the first two days after it was launched, with some videos viewed more than two million times by the war's end.[44] The military deemed its efforts a categorical success, and the virality of the footage would undergird subsequent military decisions to substantively expand the work, objectives, and scale of its social media unit.[45]

The state and its satellites also turned to Twitter during the course of the incursion, experimenting with a platform that would prove vital to state PR in subsequent years.[46] The Israeli consulate in New York opened its own Twitter account two days after the start of the Israeli offensive, followed by a Twitter-based press conference—another "first time" heralded

FIGURE 2.3. SANITIZING THE BOMBARDMENT, YOUTUBE, 2008–2009. Military footage of Israeli strike. SOURCE: https://www.youtube.com/user/idfnadesk

by the global media. Many social media pundits on both the political left and right criticized the state's efforts, drawing attention to the awkward fit between a "propagandistic" agenda and a social media platform embraced for its supposed transparency.[47] Others castigated the state for its "ham-handed" use of popular platforms, for failing to understand the norms of social media engagement and therein compromising the political message.[48] The Israeli consulate and Israeli media would laud this technological innovation, insisting that Twitter had "revolutionized Israeli diplomacy" through its unprecedented state use of micro-blogging for diplomatic purposes.[49]

Cast Lead was a watershed as far as digital militarism was concerned. In addition to the military's advance into the field of social media, this was another moment of mass civilian conscription of new media technologies for militarized ends. But unlike the earlier cyberbattles, relatively small in scale and dependent on technical knowledge, this conscription involved large numbers of ordinary citizens who were employing everyday social media tools as their vehicles, logging on from their home computers to argue the state's case before global online audiences.

The Freedom Flotilla and Its Lessons

The 2010 Israeli military assault on the Freedom Flotilla—a naval convoy carrying humanitarian aid and hundreds of international activists who aimed to break Israel's blockade of the Gaza Strip—was the next landmark.[50] The Flotilla's journey to Gaza generated massive mobilization on social media, producing a crowded political playing domain in which anti-occupation activists, patriotic Israeli citizens and their global supporters, and Israeli state officials all employed new media to advance their respective political messages.[51] Although failing to reach Gaza's shores and break the blockade, and despite military efforts to produce a total media blackout, Flotilla activists claimed a social media victory.[52] The organizers tweeted updates from the boat, webcasted live with cameras uplinked to the Internet and satellites for simultaneous rebroadcasting, and employed social networking websites to enable the public to follow them in real time. A quarter-of-a-million users viewed their Livestream videos alone.[53] The Israeli seizure of the naval convoy, resulting in the deaths of nine activists and numerous casualties, would go viral, attracting thousands more.[54]

For the Israeli military, the episode was deemed a colossal public relations failure, this despite efforts to employ social media platforms to state advantage in the operation's midst and aftermath. As earlier, YouTube was their platform of choice, with new videos released every few hours, three ranking among YouTube's most viewed during the period in question, while military tweets and blogs provided steady updates.[55] Yet for the military, social media use engendered as many problems as it solved. The IDF had waited hours after the initial confrontation at sea to release the "grainy but distinct footage it had been sitting on all day"—of the Navy commando night descent. In that window of delay, many argued, the public relations war had been lost.[56] And it was soon revealed that the military's YouTube footage had been seized from onboard activists and journalists, then edited and captioned to tell the state's story, and controversy ensued (Figure 2.4).[57] Controversy would arise again following the military's YouTube release of a supposed audio transmission with Flotilla activists before the raid. Independent bloggers charged the army with tampering to produce a damning activist portrait, replete with Holocaust slurs and 9/11 jingoism.[58] One day later, the Israel Defense Force spokesperson was forced to issue a "correction" on its webpage, noting "questions regarding the authenticity of the recording."[59]

Israelis were also employing the Internet and social media to support their state's actions, many speaking in baldly violent tones.[60] Hundreds of Israeli online Internet users condemned the Flotilla activists, many calling for a heavy-handed armed response: "The ship should be sunk in the open sea," wrote one. "And let everyone die, so no soldier gets hurt!!!"[61] This virulent digital chorus varied from informal commentary to social media creativity and parody—all in the service of the state. The most

So Soldiers are more lives important?

FIGURE 2.4. YOUTUBE AND THE STATE'S STORY, YOUTUBE, 2010. Military footage of Flotilla operation seized from activists. SOURCE: https://www.youtube.com/user/idfnadesk

celebrated of such creative efforts was a video produced by Israeli right-wing satirists ("We Con the World") featuring Flotilla activists refigured as singing terrorists—a video viewed on YouTube over a million times in the operation's immediate aftermath (Figure 2.5). These numbers were celebrated by Israeli newspapers as a national triumph: "In a place where the official Israeli public relations failed," wrote an editorial in the daily *Yediot Aharonot,* "a popular wave has risen up and succeeded."[62]

Where digital militarism was concerned, the Flotilla episode was a turning point, and in several regards. First, it demonstrated the degree to which interactive digital sites could be mobilized as political tools of the right as well as the left—not only, that is, in the hands of anti-occupation activists, veterans in the field of digital media, but also among patriotic citizens, themselves relative newcomers to the social media field. As such, the event worked to bolster the progression of digital militarism, heightening its potential and swelling its popular ranks. At the same time, the episode proved damning for the Israeli military, illustrating its failure to use the social media toolbox adequately and effectively. In the months that followed, Israeli newspapers would discuss "the excruciating flop of the Israeli digital

[handwritten margin note: effect on public relations]

The greatest bluff of all

FIGURE 2.5. SATIRICAL PATRIOTISM, YOUTUBE, 2010. "WE CON THE WORLD."
SOURCE: https://www.youtube.com/user/LatmaTV

media response"—or what some deemed later the "the Flotilla Fiasco."[63] As many Israeli pundits and journalists lamented, the state's social media efforts were both belated and inadequate. One Israeli journalist articulated the objections succinctly: "For a country so technologically advanced, and with such acute public diplomacy challenges, to fail so miserably at preparing a communications offensive over new media is a failure of strategic proportions."[64]

In subsequent months, state use of social media would be substantively reappraised. For many Israeli officials in branches of both government and military, the "Flotilla fiasco" solidified the need to take social networking more seriously, as both a tool of information dissemination and an arena of counter-insurgency. The Israeli Foreign Ministry would lead the governmental charge in this regard, cognizant of the importance of social media in the perennial battle for popular opinion. In doing this, the Ministry argued, standard idioms of state talk needed to be dramatically transformed. One senior spokesperson articulated the matter this way:

> It is clear to us that messages that pass through the social media need to be simpler, to be based on elements with international authority. For instance, it isn't enough to say there's a maritime blockade—we have to explain where it can be under international law. Since the explanation is a complex legal one, which contradicts the simplicity of messages by Twitter or Facebook, we have to distill the complex messages in a more accessible way, and send links to legal sources.[65]

"Accessibility" would become a hallmark of the subsequent Israeli state investment in social media—fueled by a belief in the uniquely persuasive powers of this popular field of mass communications.[66] The Foreign Ministry's new approach to social media contrasted sharply with prior military use of networking platforms, particularly the investment in didactic YouTube broadcasts of the state's wartime message (replete with captions and arrows to control the image).

In the months and years that followed, state bodies would substantively increase their engagement with social media tools and platforms: bolstering anti-hacking defenses;[67] expanding their monitoring of anti-occupation activities, particularly among Palestinian populations;[68] increasing their courtship of international bloggers able to defend Israel's image online;[69] and endeavoring to gain a stronger foothold on popular social media platforms and digital spaces via "likes," "shares," and numbers of followers. But most crucially, this period would mark a shift in the state's relationship to social media. Now, both the Israeli government and military would attempt to inhabit social media platforms as fictively ordinary and everyday users, transforming the traditionally formalized and hierarchical language of state talk and press releases into the popular terms required by Twitter and Facebook, where informality was at a premium.[70] In the process, the state was attempting to transform itself into a vernacular player in the digital battlefield. This everyman profile was thought to hold considerable potential as an idiom of political persuasion, one particularly crucial during times of war.

Pillar of Defense:
The Rise of Personalized Militarism

When Israel launched operation "Pillar of Defense" in November 2012, its social media arsenal was ready. In the early hours of the military campaign, the eyes of global audiences were turned to Israel's "first time" deployment of social media platforms as wartime instruments. Such technophilia notwithstanding, a substantial shift in the domain of Israeli digital militarism was at work. In years past, the military had chiefly employed the Internet for counter-insurgency or as a broadcast medium for didactic messaging. In 2012, the military would employ social media very differently. During the course of the incursion, platforms such as Facebook and Twitter became wartime tools in their own right, transformed into so-called "technologies of warning" and warfare declaration.[71] The contrast with the 2008–2009 campaign was, many pundits argued, striking. From many media corners, the military was congratulated for improving the efficacy, scale, and timing of its social media engagement.[72]

During Pillar of Defense, ordinary Israeli and pro-Israeli civilians were also employing social media in new ways, the culmination of a process that began during the 2008–2009 Israeli Gaza incursion. While Hamas and the IDF traded public relations quips, digital pro-Israeli groups were using social media platforms to share patriotic testimonials, to voice hatred toward anti-war "traitors," to track sites of wartime devastation within Israeli territory, and to employ hashtags to catalyze solidarity (#PrayforIsrael), all capitalizing on the narrative of Israeli victimhood.[73] Now, social media platforms were dominated by patriotic right-wing groups who used networking tools to articulate and perform their fidelity to nation and state. Facebook was a particularly active locus of militarized patriotism. Many Israelis contributed to a Facebook project, "Israel Under Fire!" orchestrated by the Israeli Ministry of Public Diplomacy and run by Israeli volunteers (Figure 2.6).[74] Others established similar grassroots initiates of their own. All received praise from the nation's highest office.[75] These initiatives favored private and personal modes of solidarity—foregrounding personal testimonials and ordinary portraits: handwritten Hebrew signs ("Stop the rockets"); amateur photographs from the bomb shelter; selfies with personal testimonials (Figure 2.7).[76] Such trends were also evident among soldier populations who coupled the conventional Israeli iconography of nationalism with personal gestures.

This developing trend of everyman digital militarism, itself a by-product of global networking trends, had a parallel in the military's emerging social media strategy—one focused on the embrace of ordinary networking conventions. The military's most viral material, most covered by the global media (for example, its Facebook poster of an "eliminated" Hamas leader), aimed to speak in the casual grammar that social media demanded and often adopted popular cultural and cinematic aesthetics as a means to reach global youth audiences.[77] In this vernacular vein, the military invited its Facebook followers to employ "likes" and "shares" as modes of militarized affect, thereby transforming standard social media protocols: "Share this if you agree that Israel has the right to self-defense" (Figure 2.8);[78] "Share the reality of life in southern Israel, share the truth";[79] "Like if you love the Israeli army."[80] In keeping with the global lingua franca, and the desire to reach international audiences, most were in English, and many employed explicit comparisons between Israel and the West.

In both official military content and the social media work of everyday Israeli users, personalized militarism was taking hold—a trend that had begun among immigrant bloggers and was now spreading. On social networks, this idiom was fast assuming the center of Israeli patriotic politics, seizing the place once occupied by nationalist ideology and instrumental political didacticism.

FIGURE 2.6. "ISRAEL UNDER FIRE," FACEBOOK PAGE I, 2012. Personal modes of solidarity with Israeli war efforts. Hebrew signs read: "Be strong." "We are with you." SOURCE: https://www.facebook.com/IsraelUnderFireLive

FIGURE 2.7. "ISRAEL UNDER FIRE," FACEBOOK PAGE II, 2012. Sign reads: "Stop the rockets, please" (in Hebrew). SOURCE: https://www.facebook.com/IsraelUnderFireLive

Comparison w/ the West

FIGURE 2.8. ISRAELI MILITARY, FACEBOOK CAMPAIGN, 2012. "What Would You Do?"
SOURCE: https://www.facebook.com/idfonline

Militarization and Public Secrets

The period just described was one of growing digital literacy on both the national and global scale, years in which mobile technologies were spreading at rapid rates. In the process, social media became a crucial—if not *the* crucial—locus of pro-Israeli militarized dialogue, performance, and mobilization among Israeli populations and their international supporters.

Several shifts were at the core of these developments: shifts in user demographics, strategy, and the form and content of the militarized engagement. The demographic shift was perhaps the most marked. The field of digital militarism progressed from a small constituency of computer-savvy youths to the mass mobilization of everyday social media users, a militarized population who quickly outnumbered Israeli anti-occupation activists, veterans of the politicized Internet. In 2008, they would be joined by officials from the Israeli military. And the military presence would grow dramatically in the ensuing years, progressing from improvisational efforts to a substantial state investment in carefully honed social media campaigns. Shifts in strategy and form ran parallel to these changes. Hackers had required computer expertise to mount their interventions. Israeli social media users, by contrast, employed the everyday social media protocols and conventions at their disposal. In the early years of their mobilization, patriotic militarism was expressed as sporadic responses to anti-Israeli sentiment, usually in online forums or website comments. Such responses became increasingly proactive and aggressive during the social media age, as these networked communities became more organized and militarized. By 2012, the most banal of social media practices and gestures—"likes," "shares," memes, and selfies—had been harnessed as a means of supporting state violence. In sharp contrast to the days of hacktivism, when the message had been a secondary part of the political intervention, these users worked creatively with social media wit, image protocols, and rhetorical conventions to articulate their political stance.

The ascendance of a personalized idiom was at the core of these recent developments, a form of digital militarization predicated on social media informality, casual address, autobiographical idioms, and mobile self-portraits. The roots of such developments can be traced to the 2008–2009 Israeli military campaign on the Gaza Strip, when Israeli civilians began deploying autobiography and personal testimonies as wartime PR. This trend would intensify during the 2012 assault on Gaza, when large numbers of Israeli civilians adopted personalized narrative as a means of supporting the incursion. And even as ordinary citizens were harnessing their personal lives to political campaigns, the Israeli state was laboring to speak in the vernacular language of the social media everyman—a lesson learned from the failures of traditional forms of didactic and hierarchical state talk during prior military operations.

In many ways, the shift toward personalization replayed the logic of the "first time" narratives that framed digital militarism throughout. This storyline installed the fiction of temporal novelty, collapsing history into an all-consuming present, a story contingent on perpetual forgetting of the past. Personalized militarism engaged in a similar process, a similar logic of collapse. Here, the state and its violence were reduced to the individual, even as military operations were represented as personal projects via family pictures, handwritten placards, and private moments of civilian life "under fire."[81] Together, these interlinked processes acted as technologies of public secrecy, that process of agreeing not to know the violence of occupation in social media times. Personalization masked state violence through the patina of the private, while "first times" obscured its working through historical amnesia. All of these social media tools and storylines functioned to mask the brutality of the Israeli war machine.

By the end of Israel's 2012 military incursion, the last military campaign documented in this chapter, social media had been fully integrated into Israeli war and occupation efforts; by 2014, as evidenced during the Gaza incursion of that year, the integration of these digital tools into military contexts would be surpassed by their normalization as military tools—a process we describe in the chapters that follow. What these developments make clear is the dynamic nature of the techno-political field in question. They illustrate the extent to which digital militarism is not a static entity but rather a process of ongoing militarization, highly changeable and dynamic, shifting in accordance with changes in the political, technological, and social terms of the Israeli landscape. Through these developments, which conjoined state and civilian actors within a shared domain, new practices and grammars of military occupation emerged. Through these developments, new modes of state violence were in the making.

3

Anatomy of a Facebook Scandal
Social Media as Alibi

"As an IDF spokesman, I can assure you that the act in no way reflects the spirit of the IDF or the ethical code to which we all aspire. . . . The spirit of the IDF is our policy, not shameful photos on Facebook."

IDF Spokesperson, 2010[1]

"This is commonplace. Don't you take pictures of your everyday life? For these soldiers serving in the occupied territories, this is what they see 24/7: handcuffed and blindfolded Palestinians."

Yehuda Shaul,
Breaking the Silence, 2010[2]

"I have pictures that are far worse. . . . Her mistake was that she put them on the Internet."

Israeli online commentator
responding to the Abergil affair, 2010[3]

IN THE SUMMER OF 2010, Israeli bloggers stumbled upon the Facebook account of a former Israeli soldier named Eden Abergil, their attention drawn to an album titled "IDF, the best days of my life," enhanced with a smiling emoticon.[4] At first glance, the contents of the album appeared unremarkable: pouting portraits with sunglasses and uniform; casual snapshots with friends and military jeeps; uniformed colleagues smiling for the photographer in office interiors. But buried in this commonplace catalogue of everyday life on a military base was a set of more notable images that shocked the Israeli public in 2010: snapshots

FIGURE 3.1. "THE BEST DAYS OF MY LIFE" I, FACEBOOK, 2010. Former Israeli soldier Eden Abergil posing with Palestinian detainees. SOURCE: http://sachim.tumblr.com

of Abergil posed playfully against the background of three blindfolded Palestinian men seated on cement blocks, their hands bound with plastic handcuffs, their bodily comportment weary, the locale nondescript. In one, Abergil posed like a mock cover girl with lips pursed, bound men at her back (Figure 3.1). In another, she was seated next to a detainee, her head turned suggestively toward him, a plastic handcuff resting casually on her lap. All were fodder for a jocular conversation between Abergil and her Facebook friends, who employed standard social media syntax—abbreviations, misspellings, and playfully vernacular tone—in their sexualized reading of the scene:[5]

Friend 1: "You're the sexiest like that . . ."

Eden Abergil: "Yeah I know lol honey what a day it was look how he completes my picture, I wonder if he's got Facebook! I have to tag him in the picture! lol."

צבא..התקופה הכי יפה בחיי (: - Photos s'עדן אברג'יל

Photo 7 of 55 Back to Album · עדן's Photos · עדן's Profile   Previous Next

Added August 3

From the album:
by צבא..התקופה הכי יפה בחיי (:
עדן אברג'יל

Share
Tag This Photo
Report This Photo

Adi Tal (:..הכי סקסי לך ככה
August 4 at 10:05am · Flag

עדן אברג'יל כן אני יודעת חח ואו אמא איזה יום זה היה תראי איך הוא
משלים לי את התמונה,מעניין אם יש לו פייסבוק אני חייבת לתייג אותו
בתמונה! חחח
August 4 at 11:31am · Flag

Shani Cohen !!!חחחחחחחח חולת נפש
....מעניין נזי הצלמתתתתתת
August 4 at 2:17pm · Flag

Shani Cohen !!!עדן... עומד לו עלייך.. חחחח בדוקו
August 4 at 2:17pm · Flag

עדן אברג'יל חחחח לא כפרה עומד לו עלייך בגלל זה צילמת את זה
!!!חחח את צילמת אותיו
August 4 at 2:18pm · Flag

FIGURE 3.2. "THE BEST DAYS OF MY LIFE" II, FACEBOOK, 2010. Translation of dialogue appears on pages 40 and 42. SOURCE: http://sachim.tumblr.com

Friend 2: "*LOL you psycho . . . I wonder who's the photographerrrrr.*"

Friend 2: "Eden . . . he's got a hard-on for you . . . lol for sure!!!"

Eden Abergil: "Lol no honey he's got a hard-on for youuu this is why you took that picture lol you took my picture!!!!" (Figure 3.2)[6]

Abergil's Facebook profile, initially unprotected by strict privacy settings, became a viral sensation among Israeli social media users and rapidly reached broader international audiences who eagerly consumed these provocative images.[7]

Although read as incendiary by most Jewish Israelis in 2010, these scenes of army degradation and aggression were not unfamiliar. Many Israelis could have recognized them from their own military service, having witnessed or been party to comparable acts. "There is no IDF soldier in a combat unit that does not have at least one photograph with cuffed detainees, blindfolds on their eyes," wrote one commentator in an online response to Abergil's album, his words echoed by many readers.[8] In addition, the Israeli photographic archive of such routine military violence was also considerable, the personal camera having long been a standard component of the Israeli army toolbox, employed on the military base and within the field of operations, in digital and analog form.[9] And for its part, the Israeli media had long covered army abuse of Palestinians in the territories, including far more violent incidents. Nonetheless, the Israeli public responded to the Facebook images with shock, and a discourse of scandal proliferated.

The timing of the Abergil exposure was critical. The album went viral two months after the deadly Israeli attack on the Freedom Flotilla, during a period of growing international calls for an investigation of Israel's fatal naval interception, vociferously condemned by the Israeli state and the Jewish public (Chapter 2). And Israelis were still reeling from the international reprobation that had followed the 2008–2009 Israeli military operation in the Gaza Strip in the form of a United Nations fact-finding mission that had accused Israel of war crimes, an accusation that most Israelis deemed both unfounded and slanderous.[10] It followed that Jewish Israelis of this period had little interest in images of Palestinian suffering or accounts of Israeli military aggression, save those framed as necessary and heroic. Abergil's images had a particularly inflammatory effect in this con-

[handwritten margin note: tool of humiliation]

text, and were regarded as dangerous contributions to the international assault on Israel's public image.

This chapter studies the viral life of this so-called scandal. In part, virality was a measure of novelty. While this was not the first social media exposure involving the Israeli security forces, it was the first time that Facebook—heretofore perceived by Israelis as a chiefly personal tool, for casual use—had functioned as a staging ground for Israeli military violence at this scale.[11] But virality was primarily a measure of public anxiety in this moment of national insecurity, a measure of the national investment in managing the damning scandal. Management took the form of a project of refiguration: a public discourse that labored to characterize and explain Abergil's photographs as *something else*, something other than the violence of Israel's occupation. Israeli networked publics would mobilize in large numbers after the initial Facebook exposure in the service of this goal.

To understand the virality of this scandal, and the mass Israeli investment in its refiguration, we return to the notion of the *public secret*: something that is known but concealed, understood but protected (Chapter 1).[12] We propose that the social life of the Abergil affair illustrates how the Israeli military occupation has functioned as the nation's public secret, a normative structure of *agreeing not to know that which everyone knows* about the violent terms of Israel's military rule even as it highlights the central role of social media in secrecy prevention in the digital age. As the term's dyadic structure (at once public and secret) makes clear, the public secret is predicated on a set of oppositions: exposure and concealment, the expected and the scandalous. During the viral social life of the Abergil affair, these oppositions were repeatedly on display. In the discourse surrounding her Facebook images, the occupation appeared as both Israeli common knowledge and Israel's dirty secret. And although the event was viral, receiving voluminous Israeli media coverage for weeks and months after the original exposure, it never precipitated a national conversation about Israeli state violence. Rather, the national discussion about the affair would focus elsewhere: on matters of information security in the digital age, on social media best practices, on the lures of the Internet for those in the armed forces. Thus, within the Abergil discourse, social media functioned as some-

[handwritten marginalia: refocus: problem = digital media itself]

thing of a surrogate. To keep public secrecy intact, Israelis refocused on digital media itself, rendering this the locus of scandal. In the process, state violence receded from view.

The Scandal and Its Publics

The virality of the Abergil affair was nearly immediate. After their initial exposure, her photographs sparked nothing less than "a web storm" (as per one Israeli commentator) on Israeli social networks and Internet discussion forums. The national conversation then moved to the traditional media, filling radio airways and primetime television talk shows, generating debates among military spokespersons, anti-occupation activists, and national politicians from across the political spectrum.[13] Interviews with Eden Abergil herself proliferated throughout the public life of the scandal, featuring her avowed confusion about both the national interest in the images and the nature of her offense. "I never humiliated them," she said in the widely publicized interview she had given to the military's radio station, "I don't understand what is wrong. I took those pictures without any intent."[14] Israel's left-wing critics would characterize Abergil as the latest ugly face of military occupation. But most Israeli commentators, on both the political left and right, focused on her stupidity and vulgarity; all this, they argued, had endangered Israel's international reputation and public relations efforts (*hasbara*).[15] In this prevalent storyline, the structure of violence was inverted: Israel, rather than the detained Palestinians, was represented as the scandal's true victim.

[handwritten marginalia: Israeli spun as being the victim]

The Abergil affair also had a viral life beyond Israeli borders, quickly reaching global media audiences. Palestinian politicians and public officials were particularly vocal in decrying the images as evidence of the occupation's brutality, and their remarks often made their way into the mainstream Israeli press: "This picture of an Israeli soldier enjoying humiliating Palestinian prisoners is an example of the day to day life of the Palestinian people under occupation. It indicates that occupation is a cause of suffering and humiliation for the Palestinian people every day and it is an indicator [of the ways] that occupation also corrupts the Israelis."[16] Many international pundits proposed a resemblance between

Abergil's album and the infamous Abu-Ghraib images, casting Abergil as Israel's Lynndie England.[17] International coverage of the event, particularly in the Arab world, was discussed by the Israeli media as evidence of enduring anti-Israeli cum anti-Semitic sentiment.[18] *How? Where? How?*

Israeli military spokespersons were quick to respond to the story—this at a time when the military was struggling to develop a coherent policy with regard to social media usage among on-duty soldiers. Among the army's formal statements was a YouTube video condemning the "repulsive" act and assuring the public that it "in no way, shape or form reflects the spirit of the IDF, our ethical code to which we all aspire."[19] In such statements, the language of exceptionalism was repeatedly invoked, with an emphasis on Abergil as "one bad apple", who failed to represent the nation. Indeed, army spokespersons argued, the very virality of the incident was an index of its abnormality: had such misdeeds been an everyday IDF occurrence, they suggested, nobody would have cared.[20]

Voices from the left argued strongly against the military storyline, insisting on the prevalence of such images and their roots in Israeli military culture.[21] "Abergil is no better or worse than thousands of other Israeli soldiers," some noted. "We should always remember that this, only this and nothing else, with its ignorance, naive bigotry, and blunt power-play—is the real face of our occupation of the West Bank."[22] For some, the images generated reflections on their own army service, recollections of similar incidents of violence and abuse.[23] Others pointed to the wide availability of similar images within Israeli popular and networking culture. "Such photos are nothing new," one journalist noted. "We've seen blindfolded Palestinians fed Matzas before and made to play other games."[24] "YouTube is flooded with such videos."[25] The Israeli Committee Against Torture agreed:

> [T]hese types of pictures reflect the customary norms of IDF soldiers stationed in the crossings and the treatment given to Palestinian detainees. . . . The soldier's behavior is a product of popular IDF culture which does not consider the Palestinians as human beings with their own rights. It appears the soldier who uploaded the pictures enjoyed humiliating the detainees and disregarded their right not to have their pictures published online in humiliating circumstances, without their knowledge.[26]

The activist organization Peace Now decried this "shocking evidence of the impact of the occupation on Israeli soldiers and Israeli
society"—a statement that (and here a political irony rests, given their
left-wing stance) again installed Israelis rather than Palestinians as the
occupation's chief victims.[27]
Within popular Israeli discourse about the event, the discussion of
Abergil's sexuality pervaded.[28] Many took aim at her pursed lips, bodily
comportment, and sexualized chatter with Facebook friends ("You're the
sexiest like that . . . ").[29] In keeping with Abergil's self-staging as pin-up,
such banter figured army humiliation as mutually desirable sexual contact
("he's got a hard on for you"). A Facebook solidarity campaign with Abergil reiterated this theme, calling her "the most beautiful and sexy soldier
in the IDF."[30] Other versions of this storyline employed racist language
against Mizrahi Jews (Jews from the Middle East, Asia, and Africa), producing what one Israeli blogger called "a trail of virtual slime."[31] Abergil
was called a "miserable filth," a "disgusting freha,"[32] or "arsit"—language
that merged misogyny with racial and class superiority toward Mizrahi
Jews from the Israeli periphery or inner city.[33] The frequency of the racial
idiom within everyday Israeli networked discourse about the event contrasted sharply with mainstream media discussions. There, Abergil's racial
identity was largely ignored.[34]

Digital Privacy

Much of this viral discussion focused on the matter of digital privacy,
an issue that stemmed from Abergil's open Facebook album, unprotected
by privacy settings and thus subject to mass exposure. Some Israeli commentators raised concerns about fragile confidentiality in the digital age,
asking "Is Facebook to blame?"[35] Others called for a reconsideration of social media's terms of use and debated best practices for online protection.[36]
Some argued that Abergil's online detractors, those who mined her intimate Facebook details, were also guilty of inappropriate exposure.[37] Many
mocked her for the very expectation of privacy in a networked context.[38]
The risk to army information in the social media age was of central
concern. Israeli pundits articulated this clearly (and in ways that anticipated the Edward Snowden revelations): "[g]iven the popularity of the

Internet, [the incident] again raises the issue . . . of how to prevent leakages of confidential or embarrassing information at a time when every soldier has Facebook, Messenger, and considerable desire to 'share.'"[39] Some commentators speculated that soldiers had little understanding of such risks, noting that "[m]any young web-surfers, including soldiers and former soldiers, are not aware of privacy issues" and thus might inadvertently upload sensitive content.[40] Many blamed the ill fit between a social media culture of rampant sharing and the army's security needs and encouraged better internal education within military ranks. As a partial corrective, some suggested, digital images such as Abergil's should be "classified [as] army information [and] not be seen by anyone."[41] Others disagreed: "[I]t's not like army ammunition had been photographed . . . just terrorists."[42] Throughout the long course of the viral incident, the Israeli military reassured the Israeli public that its information security remained intact, while warning soldiers about arbitrary "friending" on Facebook. In the weeks and months that followed, the IDF would announce "new strict rules for soldiers, forbidding them to post photos from military operations and bases."[43] In turn, the Israeli media provided frequent assurances to the public about military responsiveness: "IDF military intelligence has an office tasked with identifying leaks of sensitive material and can refer cases to military police, potentially leading to a criminal conviction for any soldier caught breaking information security directives."[44]

Questions of privacy arose in various forms. Digital pixilation became a political issue in its own right, centered on the question of whose face required pixilation, whose privacy merited protection. Although many Israeli media outlets had reprinted the original Facebook pictures, others had pixilated Abergil's face—a somewhat empty gesture given that her visage had rapidly achieved iconic stature. Left-wing media outlets, by contrast, had pixilated the faces of the detained Palestinians, treating this as a symbolic act of humanity restoration.[45] Unlike Abergil, they argued, these detainees never chose to publicize their photographs, nor were aware a photograph had been taken.[46] Privacy matters extended to the original Facebook commentary ("honey he's got a hard-on for youuu . . ."), much of which had been quoted wholesale on social media. Some noted that these "friends" had not consented to their exposure and that identity pro-

[handwritten annotation: concerns about privacy, confidentiality and exposure but not the occupation + the violence and content]

tection was warranted, in the form of the obfuscation of their Facebook identities and commentary. Abergil made a related argument in repeated interviews with the press, defending her actions through a defense-of-privacy logic and chiding the public for meddling in her personal affairs.[47]

What united these concerns about privacy, confidentiality, and exposure in the digital age was a widespread refusal to discuss the scene of violence or its context. For while Israeli audiences did not doubt the photographs' authenticity (as they would in many other instances; see Chapter 4), they refused to contextualize them within a broader occupation framework. They managed this problem by turning their attention elsewhere, refocusing the viral scandal on other matters. Instead of speaking about military occupation and army violence, they spoke about army information security, digital privacy, and rules of social media conduct. In this way, the scandal was acknowledged but displaced.

Social Media Vernacular

The Abergil affair prompted numerous viral remakes, remixes, and memes on social media, to various political ends.[48] The left-wing Israeli NGO Breaking the Silence published a companion album of soldier snapshots on their Facebook page, other photographs of army violence, taken by perpetrators or their friends that coupled military occupation and soldier pleasure (Figure 3.3).[49] These photographs varied in severity, including images of soldiers with bound detainees and bloodied Palestinian corpses,[50] but all were composed and performed for the lens in keeping with the standard dictates of the amateur souvenir image, replete with smiles for the cameras.[51] Titled "The Norm That [the] IDF Spokesman . . . Denies," this Facebook album contested the army's characterization of Abergil as an aberration.[52] If the Abu Ghraib resonance had been only tenuously advanced in Israeli discourse about the affair, the Breaking the Silence album rendered the parallel explicit.[53] Other creative responses would follow, and often with very different political ends. In a gesture of solidarity with Abergil herself, a Facebook group titled "We Are All with Eden Abergil" called upon former Israeli soldiers to post similar photographs from army service.[54] Snapshots proliferated, including many of manifest army abuse against

FIGURE 3.3. BREAKING THE SILENCE, FACEBOOK, 2010. Companion Facebook album of perpetrator snapshots. SOURCE: https://www.facebook.com/BreakingTheSilenceIsrael

Palestinian detainees.[55] Yet another creative project employed the web tool Twibbon and invited social media users to add Abergil's face to their profile picture (Figure 3.4).[56] Its slogan enticed with humor: "Eden Abergil is taking a picture with *you*."[57]

Memes were the most popular means of remix commentary. In the first few hours after the Facebook exposure, Abergil's pictures would be given a "meme treatment," "rehashed and imitated in all sorts of ways" by Israeli social media users who employed classic gestures of Internet wit and parodic remake as a way to intervene in the viral scandal.[58] Some memes borrowed from Internet folk culture, adding "LOL catz"-style: "I has Facebook" or, "im in ur army corrupting ur valuez." (Figure 3.5) Others played inventively with the title of Abergil's album to reframe moments of historical watershed: "The landing on the moon, the best days of my life"; "The collapse of the Berlin Wall . . . " (Figure 3.6). Some had a markedly Israeli flavor, such as images of the Tel Aviv skyline or the Israeli conquest of 1967 overlaid with Abergil's visage.[59] Others distributed

FIGURE 3.4. SUPPORT EDEN ABERGIL, TWIBBON, 2010. SOURCE: http://twibbon.com/ support/eden-abergil

FIGURE 3.5. ABERGIL MEME I, FACEBOOK, 2010. LOL catz style. SOURCE: http:// room404.net

הנחיתה על הירח. התקופה היפה בחיי

FIGURE 3.6. ABERGIL MEME II, FACEBOOK, 2010. Moon landing.
SOURCE: http://room404.net

FIGURE 3.7. ABERGIL MEME III, FACEBOOK, 2010. Facing herself.
SOURCE: http://room404.net

blindfolds to a wide range of unlikely figures: ordinary people in homes and offices, popular cartoon heroes, toys and plants, or historical figures. Perhaps the most widely circulated of such memes pictured a redoubled Abergil, a blindfolded self in the stead of the detainee (Figure 3.7).

In keeping with the global grammar of the meme, most of these creative projects eschewed standard modes of political engagement. Like the Twibbon project, their messages were rather indeterminate: Was the transposition of blindfolds onto dolls, toys, and plants a critique of the "thingification" of Palestinians or a further enactment of it? Was the introduction of Abergil into foundational historical moments a critique of occupation or a refusal to engage with its original military context? All used a substitution logic: plant for Abergil, moon landing for West Bank. However indeterminate, the very logic of substitution reiterated patriotic discourse about the scandal, a discourse predicated on replacing state violence with the discussion of something else. In this way, the conventional terms of social media parody echoed the hegemonic political field.

Scandals and Surrogates

The Abergil Facebook affair remained in the Israeli public eye for months after the initial exposure. And new information would emerge: the location and date of the original photographs (2008, Gaza Strip); the biographies of the blindfolded men; and so on.[60] Nearly a year after the incident, Abergil's Facebook page would go viral again: "Death to the Arabbbbbssss!," she wrote following the killing of a Jewish settler family in the West Bank. The military's investigation also received extensive national coverage, including news that only "disciplinary action" was deemed necessary.[61] While affirming the "disgraceful" nature of Abergil's conduct, the state prosecutor argued the inapplicability of military law in the case, as Abergil was not active military at the time of the Facebook exposure. Her photographs were declared to have no lasting military or legal relevance, no institutional implications—this in keeping with the pervasive logic of exceptionality that framed the affair (one "bad apple," one "stupid Freha").

While Abergil eventually left the Israeli headlines, other military scandals on social media would follow. They included video of an Israeli soldier dancing around a blindfolded Palestinian woman; photographs of smiling recruits, their arms around blindfolded Palestinian detainees;[62] and images of female soldiers wearing only their army-issued weapons and ammunition, posing provocatively for the camera ("giving the term Gaza Strip new meaning," in the words of the Israeli media).[63] With each successive revelation, a double and internally contradictory story-line would unfold within Israeli popular discourse: the events would be marked as exceptions even as their numbers proliferated. Official military statements would always follow, and some events catalyzed a revision or tightening of official regulations pertaining to social media engagement by members of the armed forces.[64] After each revelation, the Israeli public would again express surprise at the amorality, indecency, or stupidity of the young soldier in question, with the indiscretion explained as a matter of personal circumstance (age, familial context, or social background). In this way, the logic of exceptionality was kept intact.

In all of these subsequent revelations, the Abergil affair would be referenced.[65] Journalists would cite the Abergil case, and Israeli social media users would employ Abergil's signature phrase, sometimes in hashtag form (#bestdaysofmylife). Indeed, the Israeli social media lexicon would become *abergilized*, her terminology rendered shorthand for army indiscretions of any kind, the affair elevated to the status of Israeli cultural icon. The scandal became no less than a touchstone for all scenes of occupation exposed on networking platforms, cited endlessly whenever the informal postings of Israeli soldiers would garner media attention for their salacious tenor or inappropriate treatment of military information. And with each successive exposure, the abergilized lexicon would install her Facebook pictures as a fictive point of origin, as if this scandal, rather than a history of state violence, functioned as the precedent in question.

What, precisely, had the Abergil affair exposed where Israeli publics were concerned? As commentators continually remarked, Abergil's images were neither new nor surprising. And neither the subsequent "web storm" nor the string of subsequent social media scandals catalyzed an Israeli conversation about broader issues: army violence, the occupation's Palestinian victims, or Israeli responsibility for them. Rather, the national conversation had focused on other things: on social media protocol in a time of information insecurity, on the dangers of indiscriminate uploading, on the careless social media practices of Israeli youth. Although the public urged a shift in Israeli military policies regarding social media use, with calls for better internal education within military ranks to safeguard information security, there were few calls to reassess soldier behavior or military policy in the occupied territories.

In these national conversations, then, matters of social media and digital technology functioned as surrogate centers. The debates worked through replacement, whereby the emphasis on matters of technology— information security and digital privacy, social media rules and best practices—supplanted and obfuscated the occupation's violence. In the process, social media were installed as the chief offender. As one probing headline put it, "Is Facebook to Blame?"[66] In the process, Palestinian victims of army abuse were obscured by Israeli victims of privacy infringement. This was not simply a case of *agreeing not to know* the violence of occupation. Here, Israelis were *agreeing to know it as something else*. One Israeli online commentator put the matter succinctly: "I have pictures that are far worse[. . . .]Her mistake was that she put them on the Internet."[67] Abergil's chief offense, in the eyes of many commentators, was her failure to prevent the images' circulation. As such, social media were framed less as the scandal's platform than the root of its violence, less its medium than its content.

The Abergil affair was merely one instance in the long Israeli history of public secrecy and its exposures. Still, it is suggestive of the ways that social media have altered the secrecy economy more broadly, requiring a shift in its terms and strategies. When viral circulation, rather than army actions, functions as the locus of violence, social media work not to expose but to excuse. In this rendering, social media figure not only as the culprit, but also as the occupation's new alibi.

4

Palestinians Who Never Die
The Politics of Digital Suspicion

> "A dead man came to life in Gaza!"
>
> *Israeli blogger charging Palestinians*
> *with a staged death, 2012*[1]

> "CNN's Anderson Cooper recently apologized for using footage in which a person who appeared to be dead was 'not quite as dead a few moments later,' the Jewish Agency representative quipped."
>
> *The Jerusalem Post, 2012*[2]

"A TIP: HOW TO RECOGNIZE A FAKE PHOTOGRAPH." Such was the title of a short article that appeared in the new media supplement of the Israeli daily newspaper *Haaretz*.[3] Working slowly and meticulously through digital sources, its author provided concrete strategies for detecting social media manipulations and Internet frauds, including tips on mining metadata to detect alterations, tools for image testing, and so on. The article was unremarkable by most measures, these and other strategies being common in the age of frequent digital image manipulation. But what distinguished the text was its political framework, as its subheading made clear: "Some simple tests to avoid the mistake [made by] the BBC reporter who thought that a wounded Syrian child was photographed in Gaza."[4]

The episode was well known to Israeli readers. Indeed, at the time of this publication in 2012, it had acquired iconic status in Israeli popular imaginations. At issue was a photograph that went viral on social media during the course of Israel's 2012 military campaign in the Gaza Strip—a photograph tweeted by Hamas' Al Qassam Brigades, showing a weeping father cradling the body of his child as doctors looked on. Thanks to the diligent work of an amateur Israeli sleuth, it was revealed that the photograph had actually been shot in Syria several weeks prior, having been repurposed by Hamas for political gain (Figure 4.1). News of the discovery went viral on Israeli social networks, including an image of the Hamas tweet, alongside a screengrab of the original photograph as it had first appeared on Facebook. This was, many Israelis argued, irrefutable evidence of the deceitful and corrupt nature of both Palestinian and global media campaigns against Israel. The *Haaretz* article, published one day after the end of Israel's military operation in Gaza, was meant as a political rather than a merely technical toolbox, a means for Israelis wounded by a manipulative global media to detect defamation in Photoshop guise.

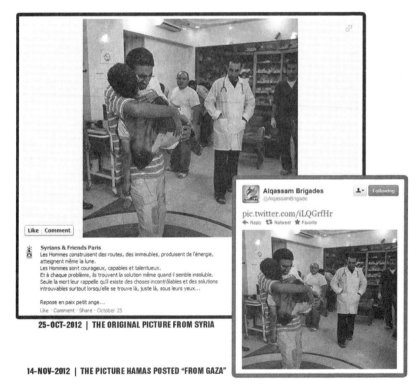

FIGURE 4.1. DOCTORING ACCUSATION I, FACEBOOK, 2012.
SOURCE: http://www.jewishjournal.com/israelife/item/hamas_lies_exposed

In the eyes of many Israelis, such digital manipulations were at the heart of the international condemnation of Israel's actions in the Gaza Strip in 2012, condemnation framed in the language of human rights but constructed, so many contended, on fabricated stories and questionable archives. To substantiate their claims, they pointed to the slew of wartime images circulated on social media during the course of the military campaign—chiefly of dead or severely wounded Palestinians, victims of Israeli airstrikes. They argued that most were fakes, their content staged, Photoshopped, or shot somewhere else and placed into circulation by Israel's foes (pro-Palestinian or anti-Semitic individuals or groups). The Israeli perception of the war's visual field was dominated by this kind of suspicion directed toward Palestinians and the international social media community.

Suspicion also shaped the social media participation of many Israeli users and their international supporters during the course of the 2012 Gaza assault; many engaged in fraudulence detection and exposure as a means of patriotism. Some immersed themselves in the scrupulous work of digital forensics, investigating metadata, charting the play of light and shadow within an image to expose digital manipulation (in keeping with the *Haaretz* template). Far greater numbers spread suspicion in less technical and arguably more effective ways, making use of standard social media tools and narrative registers: "likes," "shares," and reposts of the fraudulence charge; website commentary; and personalized outcries. These suspicious readers were praised by Israeli state spokespersons for defending the country by protecting truth—this in sharp contrast to an enemy "that prides itself on lies," in the words of an Israeli official from the Jewish Agency, a pro-state NGO.[5] In state and popular rendering, suspicious readings and digital detection were nothing less than defensive acts, means of protecting Israel from unscrupulous detractors in this time of "war."

While Israeli patriotism by means of suspicion was heightened during the course of the 2012 Gaza campaign, it was hardly new to this moment. Rather, within the broader settler-nationalist context, the Israeli right has long mobilized suspicion as a means of refusing various Palestinian political and historical claims: indigeneity, land ownership, histories of Israeli violence. Israeli suspicion of this kind has been most forcefully rehearsed in relation to 1948, mobilized as a way to invalidate Palestinian testimonials about their forcible expulsion and dispossession, thereby cleansing Israel of responsibility for the Palestinian refugee population.[6] And such forms of Israeli patriotic suspicion have also proliferated in the face of more recent Palestinian testimonials about Israeli-inflicted violence and repression in the contemporary occupation context, suspicion that often centers on the presumed unreliability of Palestinian eyewitnesses.[7]

Tethering suspicion to the image—still or moving—is unique neither to Israel nor to the social media context. As numerous scholars of photography have discussed, debates about photographic authenticity are as old as camera technologies themselves, debates that are often heightened in war contexts.[8] But the age of digital media, with the growth and spread of new technologies, has produced a marked shift in the tenor and scale of such debates.[9] It has witnessed the emergence of what we term *digital suspicion*—a mode of suspicion directed against the digital image and archive as such, articulated most prominently on social media, often in the language of amateur digital forensics (in charges of digital doctoring, Photoshop manipulation, and so on). In 2012, at the time of this Israeli military operation, suspicion of this kind had become a commonplace dimension of social media literacy on the global scale.[10] Indeed, among many social media publics, it had become a default reading strategy.[11]

The discourse of digital suspicion was mobile geographically and politically. In the Israeli context, it was deployed by a wide variety of Israeli political communities and for highly varied political ends. At times, it was used by anti-occupation activists working to challenge and destabilize the state's hegemonic truth claims, but it was also employed by the Israeli right and its international supporters to support state projects. By 2012, the time of the "Pillar of Defense" operation in Gaza, digital suspicion was predominantly the domain of right-wing, patriotic, and militantly nationalist groups. It had become a privileged grammar and discourse by which ordinary Israeli patriots, both inside and outside the country, could articulate their support of Israeli state military projects. For these communities, suspicion was at once a form of knowledge and an affective disposition—a way of securing their Zionist political claims and identities, and of producing the structures of feelings and community ties on which

dimension of social media literacy:
Suspicion → for political ends

such claims depend. And in months and years hence, the discourse would grow and proliferate as a tactic of digital militarism.

By 2012, digital suspicion had been seamlessly recruited into the project of pro-Israeli patriotic militarism—a process by which the familiar globalized social media language of suspicion had been tethered to the long-standing Israeli disbelief of Palestinian political claims. What emerged through this coupling was a *new modality of militant patriotism*—one chiefly articulated through the language of technical competence. Social media became the chief arena in which suspicion claims were mobilized, scrutinized, and assessed. It was on social media that suspicious networked publics gathered in large numbers to make their arguments and marshal their technical evidence, recruiting supporters and waging political interventions in the rhetoric of deceit and exposure.

Our analysis does not lay claims to the truth or falsehood of any particular suspicion charge. Rather, we are interested in the form, scale, and political force of the suspicion charge itself. At the core of this chapter is a concern for the ghostly figure on which this charge turned: the Palestinian victim of Israeli military assaults.[12] Public secrecy in Israel typically works by obfuscating the Palestinian victims of state violence. In the discourse of digital suspicion, by contrast, we see the victims placed at the story's center—but with a difference. In the suspicion storyline, the Palestinians in question appear not as injured or dead human beings but as pixels; not as fleshy bodies, but as dubious content. The language of digital suspicion in the hands of pro-Israeli patriotic communities transformed the prevailing logic of secrecy, rearticulating it through the figure of the fictive victim and securing its political ends through the vocabulary of digital deceit.

This is extremely dangerous

Digital Suspicion and Its Histories

At the turn of the twenty-first century, prior to the advent of social media, one shocking episode of Palestinian death at Israeli army hands would become the focus of a pro-Israeli suspicion campaign at an unprecedented global scale. The event was the infamous killing of twelve-year-old Mohammed al-Dura in Gaza during the very first days of the second Palestinian *Intifada* in 2000—a period characterized by a heavily

[handwritten: beginning of 2nd intifada]

militarized Israeli response to mass demonstrations across the occupied territories, backed by an Israeli public disenchanted by the collapse of the
Oslo process and beginning their collective move to the political right.[13]
The killing was captured on video; the resultant stills circulated widely
on both Israeli and international television screens in the days that followed, becoming what many media pundits deemed the uprising's most
iconic images. But what most international viewers saw as a scene of IDF
violence, many right-wing Israeli viewers and their international propo-
nents read as hoax, arguing that the boy's death was staged for the camera
by a crew eager to defame the Israeli military—a suspicion charge which
rested on the claim of politically motivated editing and on-site theatrics for
the camera. Over a decade later, in 2013, the Israeli government officially
embraced the hoax hypothesis, calling the al-Dura affair and subsequent
international condemnation of the Israeli army a "modern-day blood libel
against the State of Israel."[14] A pro-Israeli suspicion campaign on a similar
scale would emerge following the Israeli incursion into Jenin of 2002, the
largest Israeli military operation in the West Bank since the 1967 war.[15] In
this case, Palestinian claims of a massacre by the Israeli army, coupled with
vociferous international condemnation of Israeli military actions, catalyzed
voluminous denial among Israeli communities. In the absence of damning
images of the events, this suspicion campaign initially took aim at Palestinian eyewitness testimonials,[16] later targeting a documentary film chroni-
cling the events.[17]

[handwritten left margin: when the death of a Palestinian is seen as a bigger wound to the State of Israel]

But *digital* suspicion would emerge several years later in accordance
with shifts in the technological playing field, including the populariza-
tion of image modification tools (Photoshop chief among them). The
charge was first leveraged to viral effect during the 2006 war between
Israel and the Lebanese Shi'i movement Hizballah, what some Israeli
journalists would term the "first Photoshop war."[18] During and following
the wartime violence, pro-Israeli U.S. bloggers would accuse professional
journalists of staging scenes of Lebanese casualties for the camera and
of rampant image manipulation designed to inflate the scale of Israeli
aggression.[19] Most famous among these was the case of the Lebanese
journalist who "used software to distort an image of smoke billowing
from buildings in Beirut," an image and charge that went viral in the
global media.[20] After the initial exposure, Israeli journalists and blog-

gers engaged in heavy scrutiny of other wartime photographs, pouring through published images with an eye to fraudulence and camera-ready theatrics, particularly Lebanese "playing dead" for the camera.[21] They argued that many such scenes of fraudulence could be found ("Man seen 'dead' in Beirut photo essay appears in other photos from same scene up and walking around," in the words of one Israeli newspaper).[22]

A sarcastic disregard of Lebanese casualties became commonplace in the mainstream Israeli media of that time. All dead bodies were subject to suspicious readings, all casualty statistics in doubt. Such national sentiment swelled following the deadly Israeli air strikes on the Lebanese village of Qana, which resulted in the death of at least twenty-eight Lebanese civilians, many children among them.[23] As images of dead Lebanese children circulated in the global media, pro-Israeli bloggers again raised the suspicion charge, arguing that civilians were posing dead to increase the body count: "How do you introduce new bodies into the scene of a bomb strike?" asked a U.S. blogger quoted in the Israeli media. "The answer may be as simple as you bring them from around the corner."[24] Media manipulation had become a default anti-Israeli tactic exercised by state foes, Israeli journalists argued, a global effort to inflate the picture of Israeli violence and harm Israel's national image. "Digital forgery," they argued, "has become the norm."[25]

The form of the suspicion charge, and the identity of the suspicious reader, would shift markedly during the Israeli military assault on the Gaza Strip in 2008–2009. In 2006, professional journalists and bloggers had led the suspicion charge, often substantiating their claims through professed expertise in digital forensics. But in 2008–2009, these charges were also advanced by ordinary Israeli Internet users.[26] As before, bodies were their targets—in particular, the graphic photographs of Palestinian injury and death that were circulating on Internet sites and social networks (images notably absent from the Israeli national media of the moment, with its near exclusive focus on images of Israeli suffering). Some Israeli networked publics marshaled the claim of digital doctoring or theatrical staging, arguing that such technical tools had been employed by Palestinians or their supporters as a means of emotional warfare, to manipulate world opinion through fabrication or exaggeration where Palestinian casualties were concerned.[27] Others aimed their disbelief at claims about the use of white phosphorus, targeting testimonies and photographs circulated on the Internet by doctors and human rights workers based in Gaza, including photographs depicting the debilitating injuries inflicted by Israeli use of this illegal chemical weapon. (At first denied by Israel, the use of phosphorus was later described by the IDF as a mere smokescreen and eventually discontinued because, as the military noted in a concession to the suspicious public, "it doesn't photograph well" and results in unnecessary public relations damage.)[28] These suspicion charges were bolstered by well-worn Israeli propaganda that attributed all such images to anti-Semitic bodies in Europe and the Arab World.

Unbelievable

But suspicion was a highly mobile discourse, as we have suggested, its politics shifting in accordance with the populations who deployed it. During the period we have outlined, this charge was also marshaled by anti-occupation activists, both Israelis and internationals, who used suspicion to critique the Israeli state. During the 2008–2009 Gaza campaign, for example, many took aim at Israeli military videos of the aerial bombardment, videos shot from the vantage of the weapon and uploaded onto the military's nascent YouTube channel. In one well-publicized instance, Israeli and international human rights organizations challenged military footage of "Hamas rockets in transit." Disputing state claims, they identified the target as a family truck carrying welding equipment. Echoing the suspicion claims of those on the Israeli right, for whom disbelief was often rooted in close readings of the digital documents, these organizations grounded their claims in scrupulous analysis of the YouTube footage, pointing to inconsistencies between the IDF's official statements and the videos themselves.[29] Suspicion as anti-occupation tool would also be used during the 2010 Freedom Flotilla episode—with Israeli and international activists taking particular aim at the state's social media campaign to defend the naval raid (see Chapter 2). Some Israeli and international activists used amateur forensics to indict the Flickr account of the Israeli Foreign Ministry, pointing to doctored time-stamps that demonstrated (they claimed) a falsification of evidence.[30] Others raised questions about the military's YouTube content, charging the Israeli army with audio tampering to produce a doctored record of Flotilla activists. Left-wing activists would employ digital suspicion again in 2012, charging the state's YouTube and Twitter accounts with a willful "distortion" of facts (chiefly

Flotilla: Israel Foreign ministry criticized for doctored time stamps; questions about youtube content pertaining to the volume of Hamas rockets fired at Israel and the scale of ensuing Israeli casualties).[31]

As we have suggested, the landscape of digital suspicion had changed considerably during this short period (2006–2012). In 2006, in the context of the Lebanon war, suspicion was chiefly leveraged by and against professional journalists, and required authentication by means of technical explanation, often through recourse to the language of specialists (experts trained in image forensics who parsed the photograph for the unwitting public). The demand for such expertise remained active during the 2008–2009 Israeli incursion into the Gaza Strip, as computer-savvy Internet users touted their ability to distinguish authentic images from fakes on the basis of abundant technological clues, but it was beginning to erode. Gradually, the field of digital suspicion underwent vernacularization—a shift evident in both the language of the suspicion charge and the profile of the suspicious reader. By 2012, the time of the Israeli military campaign in Gaza, practices of suspicion had become commonplace within both Israeli networked contexts and broader global social media worlds. In the Israeli context, suspicion was no longer the exclusive domain of the techno-savvy but increasingly employed by a broader public: journalists and state officials, bloggers, and ordinary social media users. In the global context, stories of fakery or exposure were going viral, and the grammar of distrust was being elevated to the status of the digital everyday, an ordinary mode of dealing with networked data. In turn, the very terms of this language and hermeneutic practice were becoming codified and schematized, through a regulation of ways of seeing and evaluating data. Suspicion was becoming a publicly recognized and regulated grammar with its own vocabulary, its own terms of interpretive engagement.

Suspicion by affiliation

Dead Men Walking

By the time of the Israeli military offensive of 2012, digital suspicion was tethered closely to one particular Israeli political project: that of patriotic militarism, employed by loyal Israeli citizens and their international supporters as a defense of the state. In the hands of militant patriots, suspicion functioned as both a refutation of Palestinian political claims and a reaffirmation of the terms of Israeli military rule. This discourse was at the forefront of nationalist mobilization on Israeli social networks—working hand in hand with the personalized conscription of social media tools and the state's adoption of the social media vernacular (outlined in Chapter 2).

This political mobilization of suspicion was evident in the first hours of the 2012 Israeli offensive. As photographs and videos of Israeli-inflicted destruction in the Gaza Strip filled social networking sites, patriotic users began their work of detection, of sorting fact from fiction, encouraging others across the globe to join them.[32] Pro-Israeli Facebook groups bombarded followers with warnings about Hamas propaganda, unmasking lies through careful parsing of the images.[33] Hebrew language online commenters decried "the leftist traitors" and Israeli human rights organizations who supported and "shared" viral Palestinian deceits. Experts interviewed in the traditional Israeli media testified to the extent of the digital deception.[34] Israeli journalists and everyday users conducted feverish web research to verify digital images of wartime devastation in Gaza, employing vigilance to weed out social media fakery.[35] While some Israeli social media users lamented the loss of the wartime "real" amidst this sea of fakery, others warned fellow Israelis to beware Facebook's "share" button, lest the image in question should prove false.[36] Others focused on practical solutions, seeking to counter the numerous "Palestinian lies" with "Israeli truths": "While we have to be vigilant about anti-Israel propaganda online, it's even more important for us to spread trustful information. In particular, we should focus on spreading personal stories, photos and pictures of Israelis under fire."[37] Although these suspicious readers seized on wartime images and testimonials of multiple kinds, social media were the focus of their tribunal. Here, the case for fraudulence was paramount. Here, legions of potential suspicious readers, cum Israeli patriots, were being recruited (or this was the hope).

Among those on the militant right, one particular charge predominated: that images and videos of injured, dying, or dead Palestinians were other than they appeared. Arguments along these lines took numerous forms: that the numbers of Palestinian dead were exaggerated or falsified; that Palestinian injuries or deaths were caused by Palestinians (chiefly Hamas) rather than Israel; that Palestinian suffering and death were staged or digitally altered for the camera; or that images of dead or

who would gain from this? How many were actually repurposed?

wounded Palestinians had been repurposed, taken from other contexts. Three viral images were at the heart of this campaign against the falsified Palestinian body. The first was that of a dead child in his father's arms—the image with which the chapter began—distributed by Hamas' Twitter feed and thereafter exposed as an inauthentic duplicate.[38] The second was a BBC video of an injured Palestinian man, carried from the site of an Israeli bombing. After wide dissemination within social and traditional media (replayed repeatedly on CNN), the video was charged by pro-Israeli bloggers as fraudulent—evidence, they argued, of yet another Palestinian injury staged for the camera (Figure 4.2).[39] The third portrayed a Gazan funeral, with weeping men carrying the wrapped bodies of two small children, their deaths the result of an Israeli air strike (Figure 4.3). Selected as "World Press Photo of the Year" in 2013, it was thereafter suspected of digital modification. Alerted by the inconsistent play of light and shadow, experts in digital forensics argued that this image was a montage of several others, merged to create a single, striking frame.[40] All of these incidents generated viral discussions within Israeli media spheres, including newspapers and social media sites, online comments, and national television news programs. And all of these viral suspicion

FIGURE 4.2. DOCTORING ACCUSATION II, FACEBOOK, 2012.
SOURCE: http://www.honestreporting.ca/cbcs-oscar-worthy-pallywood-performance/67

FIGURE 4.3. DOCTORING ACCUSATION III, PAUL HANSEN, 2012. "Gaza Funeral."
SOURCE: http://www.extremetech.com

considered "heroic" + question images' authenticity

campaigns were framed as patriotic acts—no less than heroic deeds in the
online battle against Israel's defamation.

The nature and verifiability of these images varied. But in each case,
the suspicion charge was the same: these Palestinians weren't *really* dead or
injured. Rather, these casualties or deaths had been staged or digitally created for the camera. That is, what might first appear to be a dead or injured
body would be revealed as (in the sardonic language of an Israeli state official) "not quite as dead."[41] This claim rested on various kinds of evidence
and detection practices. Some readers leaned on the language of technical
expertise, their evidence based on detailed analysis of the mechanics of
deception. They pointed to incongruous perspective, angles, or lines of
light and shadow, suggestive of montage; others looked for signs of air-
brush and image editing. This techno-paranoia was particularly evident in
the debates about the funeral photograph, where the alleged use of digital
modification to merge together faces and limbs from different shots were
originally exposed by a U.S.-based forensic image analyst and then spread
by American bloggers.[42] The claims (later disproved by Word Press's own
panel of experts) then migrated to the Israeli social networks, where they

too much extrapolation

were seized upon by an eager public, their skills in digital detection having already been honed.[43]

The charge of technical forgery was, as we have suggested, at the heart of the suspicion campaign. Many readers worked closely with the images in question, scrutinizing them for signs of digital manipulation. But in 2012, another language of suspicion was now vying for centrality, representing a change from its early manifestations in 2006. Now, the technical details of the fakery began to matter less, if at all. Within a global social media sphere in which suspicion had become commonplace, now deemed a *requisite* mode of reading, many Israeli and pro-Israeli users were wasting little time with technical proof. Nor were they invested in evidence. Rather, they delivered their charges as statement of fact rather than as hypothesis, the technical details of the alleged fraud giving way to the language of political polemics. These readers sought to advance a grander and bolder fraudulence claim: arguing that the fraudulent, deceiving Palestinian was a *natural condition* that required no substantiation. This suspicion narrative, as it unfolded on social media platforms, was brash and unapologetic: "A good Arab always fakes it"; "This is no news that they fake images; they are experts [in fakery]"; "Arabs are liars by nature"; "The question is not what is a true picture, but what is a true Arab."[44] In many such narratives, the figure of the "lying Arab" quickly became a metonymy for the Palestinian nation itself: "Of course the picture [of the funeral] is fake, everything they have is fake, they are a fake People";[45] "One can expect little else from an organization that prides itself on lies. Deception is [their] way of life."[46] These readers did not need the tools of digital forensics to do their work. Their claims rested on truisms about both the image and the image makers. Both were fraudulent to their very core.

Israelis Who Never Kill

As we have suggested, the discourse of digital suspicion varied considerably during the period in question (2006–2012). It was simultaneously anchored in the language of technical proof and expertise and articulated in the form of passionate polemics that required neither evidence nor careful digital forensics. Throughout these years, and regardless of its idiom, the viral story of Palestinians who never die had a rallying effect on Israeli social media publics and their international supporters. By 2012, a time when digital fakery had become a global social media truism, the language of verification had given way to the sheer volume and force of the suspicion charge itself. In this period, suspicious readers were united in their conviction that Israeli military operations were fraudulently represented in the global and Palestinian media, fraudulence most pronounced in representations of the Palestinian dead and wounded. The global grammar of social media was thus enlisted to solve a localized Israeli political problem (or so it was perceived): the images of Palestinian deaths and injuries that circulated virally challenged the state's account of this incursion and its narrative of Israel's "existential war."[47] Suspicion reinstalled the existential threat.

As we have argued, the viral appeal of the digital suspicion storyline in 2012 was driven by the political needs of the moment. Consider, as a point of contrast, the Israeli military campaign of 2008–2009. Then, Israeli publics and mainstream media outlets paid little attention to Palestinian victims, focusing on Jewish Israeli casualities of Hamas fire. Few images of the Palestinian dead appeared in the Israeli traditional news media, print or television. They were deemed an assault on the national wartime project, particularly the state's efforts to bolster its claims about a self-defensive, no less legal, war.[48] In part, the missing Palestinian bodies of this moment were the result of Israel's media ban on the entry of Israeli and foreign journalists into the Gaza Strip—a ban aimed at controlling the wartime message and resultant field of images. And while images of death and destruction in Gaza were available on the Internet or international media, they were largely disregarded, as prevailing nationalist sentiment of the moment made little room for Palestinians' political or humanitarian claims. The 2012 incursion, by contrast, was managed very differently by the Israeli state and patriotic communities. This time, no state media ban was in place. And now, images of dead and injured Palestinians flooded the computer screens of Israeli social media users—and at precisely the moment when Israeli users were turning to social media as a mass platform for political claims. In 2008–2009, the dead Palestinian body was largely ignored and refused by Israelis. In 2012, this body occupied the political center among mili-

2008-2009—images of dead palestinans donot matter
2012 - images matter→but social media used politically→suspicion

tant patriots, conjured up by Israeli and pro-Israeli networked publics to do national work.

The conjuring of these bodies, at once dead and not-dead, brings us back to the heart of the Israeli public secret. In this act of conjuring, we return to the technology of secrecy that framed the Abergil affair (Chapter 3), whereby politics and power were replaced by social media matters, details, and technicalities. The obsession with digital forensics among many suspicious readers, with their investment in technical details of fraud detection, substituted matters of life and death with questions of technological literacy and accuracy. So although suspicion claims brought Palestinian dead bodies into visibility—in sharp contrast to the missing Palestinian body of the 2008–2009 period—these bodies were conjured not as political subjects or fleshy humans. Rather, they appeared as digital images in need of forensic dissection. Suspicious readers were managing the problem of these dead and injured bodies in new ways; not through a refusal as a means of patriotic loyalty, but through a grammar of technicality that treated human lives as a sequence of electronic records. Thus, even without military censorship, the emphasis on digital accuracy worked as a surrogate media ban, enforced not by state censorship but by everyday readers and social media consumers themselves, within the vernacular terms of global social media grammar.

Something much larger than the Palestinian body or victim was at stake. No longer limited or constrained by technicalities, the patriotic claims of 2012 were deemed a matter of ontology. Recall the words of Israeli detractors: "A good Arab always fakes it." "Arabs are liars by nature."[49] Indeed, even as some suspicious readers needed the rhetoric of digital forensics to replace the bleeding body with a digital object, many eschewed proof, taking refuge in the inherent fraudulence of *any* Palestinian claim or subject. A scalar jump was often at work in these readings: from the deceptive image to the deceptive nation, the fraudulent image figuring as both instance and evidence of the fraudulence of the Palestinian nation itself.[50] This storyline had long been at the core of settler-colonial suspicion within Israel. But in the age of social media, it had been retooled. Now it seized on the digital image as target and impetus, giving the old colonial story a new digital guise.

[handwritten note:] old colonial story → Arabs are deceptive
↳ now retooled through social media
↳ same settler-colonial suspicion

Within the terms of this storyline, the political and the technical collapsed, as matters of image authenticity folded into that of Arab authenticity. In this formula, a larger inversion was at work. The story of the fake Palestinian death figured digital fraudulence, rather than military violence, as the chief offense to which the image testified. In other words, Israeli and pro-Israeli readers understood the suspicious images as violent ones. But the violence they identified rested in neither Israeli airstrikes nor the broader regime of military occupation. Rather, it took shape in the act of image manipulation in its various guises. In the process, wartime atrocities were refigured as pixels under scrutiny. In this way, a new field of warfare was being introduced. In the estimation of suspicious readers, image manipulation became the real war crime, and social media became the court in which the crime was tried.

A similar move was at work in the Abergil affair, when social media became the occupation's ultimate alibi. But in 2012, suspicious readers took exoneration one step further. Unlike the photographs in Abergil's Facebook account, the images of dead Gazans lacked their perpetrators. The figure of the Israeli military was missing. This was more than a byproduct of Palestinian death by aerial bombardment and its visual archive. In the metonymic logic of the digital suspicion narrative, in which fraudulent body stood for the fraudulent nation, the image of the absent perpetrator functioned as a national allegory. In 2012, the story of "Palestinians who never died" was equally that of "Israelis who never killed." This was the narrative to which viral digital suspicion gestured repeatedly, and it was to this end that many Israeli patriots mined the Palestinian visual archive for traces of fraudulence. And the stakes were considerable. Framed in this way, digital suspicion cleansed not only the Israeli army of its wartime responsibility, but also the military occupation of its occupier.

5

Selfie Militarism
The Normalization of Digital Militarism

"The devices and the applications have changed. The ways in
which pictures are shared has changed. The feeling of excessive
power and the clear contempt for human life and human dignity
have remained."

Yehuda Shaul,

Israeli NGO Breaking the Silence, 2014[1]

IN 2008, a grainy video was uploaded to YouTube and tagged as
"comedy." It showed a Palestinian youth in an unidentified location, com-
plying with forced demands to perform. We watch as he sings nervously
in Arabic and Hebrew—"*Wahad hummus, wahad ful, ana behibak Mish-
mar Hagvul*" ("One order of hummus, one order of ful, I love the Border
Police"). Male voices, later identified as those of the Israeli Border Police,
bark instructions to slap himself: "Yallah, start, do it hard!" (Figure 5.1).[2]
The footage was exposed by Israeli journalists soon after its publication
and swiftly condemned by left-wing Israeli groups who called for its removal. YouTube complied, citing its guidelines on "offensive content."[3]
But the video was soon reposted under different headings, one garnering
more than ninety thousand views. The comments of many Israeli YouTube
viewers, responding in Hebrew, reiterated the "comedy" tag ("hahahaha").[4]
   The event was neither unusual nor new. Among members of the Israeli security services, there has been a long history of forcing Palestinians
to "perform," a history traceable to at least the first Palestinian uprising
(1987–1991), when such forced performances acquired an almost ritual
status among new Israeli recruits, centered on a chant ("*wahad hummus,
wahad ful*") that some Israeli left-wing pundits have called the "unofficial

אנא בחבק משמר הגבול

0:29 / 0:43

FIGURE 5.1. NETWORKED MILITAINMENT I, YOUTUBE, 2008. Israeli Border Police video of forced Palestinian performance. Reads: "I love the Border Police."
SOURCE: http://www.haaretz.com

anthem" of the Israeli occupation.[5] In the age of social media, this type of Israeli perpetrator-recorded video rapidly crystalized into a recognizable YouTube genre.[6] In such recordings, Israeli soldiers or police are typically offscreen, their voices audible but their figures missing from view. Locations are usually vague, as are the circumstances in question. At times, notes from the videographer or his companions accompany the uploaded material: "They were bored so they grabbed one guy and laughed with him and he did [the song]."[7] Often the perpetrators' pleasure is audible in sounds of laughter or off-stage commentary ("More, more!"). So, too, the terror of the Palestinian "performer"—a terror evident as foreboding silence in the song's wake.

In 2013, another scene of Israeli violence would go viral on global social networks, exposed by U.S. blogger Ali Abunimah.[8] It was a mobile snapshot of a young Palestinian boy, photographed through a sniper's crosshairs and uploaded to the Instagram account of Mor Ostrovski, a twenty-year-old Israeli soldier in a sniper unit who (it was soon discovered) had regularly used social media to document his military service in the Palestinian territories (Figure 5.2).[9] International condemnation was almost immediate, with critics decrying the dehumanizing practice of framing "Palestinian children [as] targets" regardless of their age or civilian status.[10] Others focused their ire on the image's social media provenance, its troubling interplay of digital aesthetics and militarized spectacle, of sniper logics and Instagram colors.[11] The army responded by reading from its standard script, insisting on the event's exceptional nature: "This is a severe incident which doesn't accord with the IDF's spirit and values."[12]

FIGURE 5.2. WEAPONIZED INSTAGRAM, INSTAGRAM, 2013. Image of a Palestinian boy photographed through the vantage of the sniper's rifle. SOURCE: http://electronic intifada.net/sites/electronicintifada.net

Although separated by five years, these two instances have much in common. Both are scenes of Israeli violence against Palestinians shared willfully on social media by their perpetrators. Both take Palestinian male youths as their targets, long a locus of enmity within the Israeli militarized imagination.[13] Both originally were captured on mobile phones, a consumer technology that has progressively become a requisite tool of Israeli soldiering. Both were promptly removed from the Internet following their exposures, but subsequently reposted and shared under different headings, thereby enjoying long afterlives in networked archives. And both drew on considerable histories of violence inflicted by members of the Israeli security services—violence documented, recorded, and often eagerly circulated by photographer-perpetrators. This history was highlighted by the Israeli NGO Breaking the Silence in response to the Instagram exposure. Writing on their Facebook page, they referenced a photograph taken ten years prior by an Israeli combat soldier:

> There, too, an Israeli soldier aimed a weapon at a boy and took a picture with his camera as a memento, a gesture of an endless feeling of power that is connected to control over another people . . . Ten years have passed. The devices and the applications have changed. The ways in which pictures are shared has changed. The feeling of excessive power and the clear contempt for human life and human dignity have remained.[14]

Yet the differences between these social media artifacts, between the YouTube performance and the sniper on Instagram, are also considerable. The former was a standard work of amateur videography, typical of early instances of soldier violence on the Internet. This footage was uploaded as a kind of found object, without editing or much authorial commentary. Its audiences are unaddressed; the violent force of the footage is not predicated on their presence. The militarized force of the sniper image, on the other hand, works through different routes. Here, networked spectatorship is a condition of the militarized field, integral to its workings, as the image's violence rests not only in framing the Palestinian as target, but also in its deployment of social media conventions, in the unsettling coupling of everyday digital aesthetics with militarized ways of seeing. In this second case, then, the terms of violence encompass and depend on everyday networked grammar. Violence is incorporated into the very fabric and practice of social media.

These differences illustrate the substantial transformations we have witnessed during the first two decades of the twenty-first century, years in which social media use in Israel would grow exponentially, as it would on the global scale, even as popular Jewish Israeli sentiment moved increasingly rightward. During these years, the Israeli public would consume YouTube videos of Israeli army battalions dancing in combat gear through the occupied West Bank (Figure 5.3);[15] Facebook photographs of scantily clad female recruits dancing for the smartphone, their nudity covered with army-issued weapons (Figure 5.4);[16] and increasing numbers of Israeli soldier selfies on

IDF Israeli soldiers dancing to Kesha - Tik Tok in Hebron (Rock the Casba)

283,766

🔊 Subscribe 53   👍 1,575   👎 128

FIGURE 5.3. NETWORKED MILITAINMENT II, YOUTUBE, 2010. Israeli soldiers dancing in Hebron. SOURCE: https://www.youtube.com/watch?v=xVVte55odyU

© Walla

FIGURE 5.4. NETWORKED MILITAINMENT III, FACEBOOK, 2013. Israeli soldiers stripping for the camera. SOURCE: http://inserbia.info/today/

Instagram.[17] These and other episodes conjoined social media and militaristic practices in a phenomenon we have described as *digital militarism*—a phenomenon that began fifteen years ago as the aberrant social practice of a small group of computer-savvy Israeli youths and became, by the end of this period, the domain of the social media everyman.

another definition

Today, social media function as a crucial toolbox with which civilian networked publics, inside and outside Israel, can enjoy and support their military, the politics of extremist nationalism, or both. As we have shown, social media have also become important tools in the hands of Israel's official military spokespersons, particularly during times of so-called war. But these changes in the sphere of digital militarism are not merely demographic in kind. Rather, as the examples above suggest, the very terms of this discursive field have also undergone a change. Popular networking platforms, and banal social networking gestures and genres, have become vehicles for the articulation of militarized politics and sensibilities. In the process, Israel's military rule in the Palestinian territories has extended into mundane networked domains: into the spheres of selfie aesthetics, lifestyle branding, and sharable content. Digital militarism has become the new normal.

Such developments have been dramatically evident in the changing terms of Israeli soldiering. In the first two decades of the twenty-first century, mobile technologies have become increasingly ubiquitous in military theaters. In the words of the 2014 Israeli press, young soldiers now "carry smartphones alongside their army-issued rifles" for mobile networking while on base and as tactical tools of surveillance in the field of military operations.[18] The military has struggled to keep pace with these practices, perpetually recalibrating its internal social media policy to match new media trends among this population of "digital natives."[19]

These shifts in the terms of soldiering have been evident in the evolving genre of the Israeli soldier selfie, or what we call *selfie militarism*—a genre rooted in the long tradition of military souvenir photography.[20] Today, smartphone self-portraits of smiling Israeli recruits, with or without weapons, on or off the battlefield, are flooding Israeli and global social networks. They emerged with remarkable speed: in 2012, as per the opening of this book, Israeli soldier selfies took media consumers by surprise. By 2014, in keeping with the global rise of the genre, they had become routine.[21]

Consider Mor Ostrovski, the sniper responsible for the Palestinian boy in the crosshairs. In addition to the crosshairs image, his Instagram account contained numerous militarized selfies documenting his everyday life as a combat soldier in the West Bank (Figures 5.5, 5.6). Most showed Ostrovski in army-issued uniform, often posing with weapons: between the legs as phallic prosthetic, in scenes of mock battle, or held in an embrace (Figure 5.7).[22] Some were shot in the interior of Palestinian homes, the capture of private homes being a standard feature of Israeli sniper operations (Figure 5.8). The contrast with Ostrovski's crosshairs image was striking. In his selfies, the scene of violence was relatively mundane and ordinary in form. His images contained no manifest degradation or humiliation of Palestinian subjects. Indeed, they contained no Palestinians at all—and for all these reasons, were of little interest to

FIGURE 5.5. SNIPER ON INSTAGRAM I, INSTAGRAM, 2013. Mor Ostrovski's Instagram account. SOURCE: http://electronicintifada.net/sites/electronicintifada.net/files/ostrovskimor_on_instagram.jpg

FIGURE 5.6. SNIPER ON INSTAGRAM II, INSTAGRAM, 2013. SOURCE: http://electronic intifada.net/

FIGURE 5.7. SNIPER ON INSTAGRAM III, INSTAGRAM, 2013. SOURCE: http://electronic intifada.net/

FIGURE 5.8. SNIPER ON INSTAGRAM IV, INSTAGRAM, 2013. SOURCE: http://electronic intifada.net

global audiences at the time of their exposure. In their place were Palestinian houses and landscapes emptied of their inhabitants, populated only by the Israeli security forces or their threatening shadows, images in which Israeli state violence and its Palestinian targets were replaced by the violence of erasure. In the process, a central Zionist fantasy was being replayed ("a land without a people . . ."). *excellent point → seems more like a photo shoot than a war*

As digital soldiering proliferated, selfie militarism would change in both degree and kind. Some of these developments were evident in April 2014, when an incident of routine Israeli military aggression in the occupied West Bank, filmed by a Palestinian activist, began to circulate on Israeli media channels.[23] It was a video of an Israeli combat soldier, later identified as David Adamov, caught on camera in an antagonistic confrontation with unarmed Palestinian teenagers in Hebron's old city. The content was neither new nor surprising: a soldier shoving, kicking, and pointing his gun at Palestinian youths. What was new, however, was the

form and scale of the national response. Following the soldier's suspension by the military, Israeli networked publics arose in unprecedented
numbers to support their "brother in arms"—a mass mobilization on
social media that Israeli pundits would call the military's first "digital rebellion" within its ranks, one that pitted Israeli soldiers against a military
command structure which, they argued, had failed to protect those in
its ranks against marauding Palestinian youths armed with cameras.[24] In
the days that followed, thousands of soldiers would voice their solidarity
with the detained soldier in the language of the selfie, uploading mobile
self-portraits, their faces covered by handwritten banners of protest: "We
are with David the Nahalite" (the suspended soldier was in the Nahal
Infantry Brigade) (Figure 5.9). These soldier selfies took numerous forms
(Figures 5.10 and 5.11). In some, the message of protest appeared on the
half-naked bodies of the participating soldiers. In others, it was spelled
out in ammunition or decorated with army weapons.[25] A new Facebook
group—"I, too, am with David the Nahalite"—would become their
repository.[26]

    This selfie protest would soon spread to include the civilian Israeli
public, who joined the ad-hoc solidarity movement en masse, contrib-
uting selfies shot at home and at work, with pets and mundane house-
hold objects—a protest whose sheer scale would be characterized by
the Israeli media as nothing less than a "digital tsunami."[27] Military
clarifications about the terms of the soldier's suspension, the result of
other violent instances, did not stem the ensuing tide of social media
protest. Many Israelis decried the general condition of Palestinian prov-
ocations and soldier vulnerability in the occupied territories, urging
the army to protect "the nation's children" from abandonment. Some
parents threatened to remove their sons from military service, while
soldiers condemned the military's existing "policy of restraint," arguing
that its rigid parameters left them vulnerable in the face of the hos-
tile enemy.[28] Meanwhile, military spokespersons warned of the event's
security consequences: "[If] every military or political issue provokes
an online protest from soldiers, Israeli army's power of deterrence will
pay a heavy price."[29]

    Israelis had seen much of this before: the display of patriotic soli-
darity, the narrative of soldier victimhood, and military anxiety about

FIGURE 5.9. "WE ARE ALL WITH DAVID THE NAHALITE" I, FACEBOOK, 2014. Selfies in support of an Israeli soldier disciplined by the military. Poster reads, "I am with David" (in Hebrew). SOURCE: https://www.facebook.com/Israelijustice

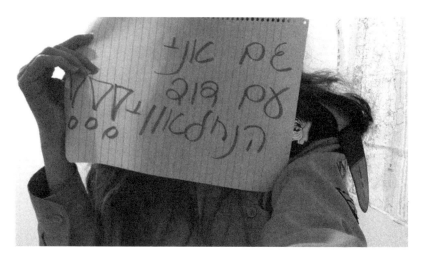

FIGURE 5.10. "WE ARE ALL WITH DAVID THE NAHALITE" II, FACEBOOK, 2014. Poster reads, "I am also with David the Nahalite" (in Hebrew). SOURCE: https://www.facebook.com/Israelijustice

FIGURE 5.11. "WE ARE ALL WITH DAVID THE NAHALITE" III, FACEBOOK, 2014. Poster reads, "I am also with David the Nahalite. We love you, David!" (in Hebrew). SOURCE: https://www.facebook.com/Israelijustice

the unfolding digital age. The public Israeli response replayed a recurrent Israeli political narrative about the military occupation—namely, an inversion whereby the armed soldier, rather than the Palestinian civilian population, is figured as its chief victim. So, too, the public support for greater military force in the face of perceived Palestinian aggression—a long-held national sentiment, but one that has emerged with renewed force since the turn of the twenty-first century, a decade and a half of growing anti-Palestinian sentiment. But something had changed. The incident was unprecedented in its scale—this being the first mass protest by Israeli soldiers on social media, no less against army policy. And in most prior instances of digital militarism, Israelis had distanced themselves from the viral "scandals" in question, treating them as aberrations or exceptions. Eden Abergil's Facebook page, Mor Ostrovski's Instagram account, the forced Palestinian performances on YouTube: all would be framed in these terms, as would many of the viral exposures that followed (the stripping female recruits on YouTube, the soldier selfies, the Facebook indiscretions). In this "digital tsunami," by contrast, Israelis were speaking differently. Rather than distancing themselves from the online scene of military violence, they were marking their solidarity with the perpetrator, joining the selfie meme en masse: *We all stand with David the Nahalite, We are all David the Nahalite.*[30]

These mass selfie protests signaled an evolution in the broader logic of digital militarism. We have argued that, during the formative years of its development (2008–2014), digital militarism was harnessed to a national project of public secrecy: namely, a project of *knowing but refusing to acknowledge as such*, or *knowing not to know*. We have employed this term to denote the willed Israeli refusal to contend with endurance of the military occupation as a political structure and the myriad ways in which Israeli military rule in the Palestinian territories shapes everyday Israeli spaces, times, and identities. In the early years of digital militarism, as this book has documented, secrecy management was paramount. The discourse of scandalous exceptionality was harnessed to this project, employed by patriotic networked publics to contain online images of Israeli military violence. The army labored to manage secrets by characterizing such incidents as breaches of its resilient ethical code, depicting them as happenstance eruptions, mere blips on the nation's mobile

beginning of period = quick to paint scandals
as exceptions, rush for
secrecy management

screens. A companion storyline would manage secrecy through conceal-ment. Indeed, many in the Israeli military would endorse this strategy as a means of preserving Israel's image. "I also have these kinds of photos," noted an army spokeswoman in 2013, following yet another exposure on YouTube (this time, videos of female soldiers stripping on an army base). "But they are locked inside an album in my storeroom."[31] The comment was both descriptive and a means of normative injunction, calling upon others to avoid embarrassing virality by keeping offending army images under lock and key, away from the unruly social media field.

As the mass selfie protests of 2014 suggest, the Israeli investment in public secrecy has evolved and changed alongside developments within the broader field of digital militarism. Now, secrets are harder to keep. Aestheticized images of Israeli soldiering have become the rule rather than the exception, an anticipated part of one's news feed or repertoire of mobile networking. Now, Palestinian victims and Israeli perpetrators routinely disappear in the hands of suspicious readers, their very presence deemed evidence of digital manipulation. And now, all Israeli military operations have a second life on computers and smartphone screens. As Israeli digital militarism has become normalized, enfolded into every-day Israeli networking practices and structures of online feeling, Israeli social media users are willingly aligning themselves with Israeli military violence. Today, Israeli civilian calls for revenge and violent retribution against Palestinians are joyfully shared on social networks, and official Israeli military spokesmen employ selfies as public relations platforms in the midst of violent Gaza incursions (Figure 5.12). As digital technolo-gies and communication platforms become increasingly widespread, as digital documents and images are increasingly subjected to viral and in-stantaneous exposure, and as greater numbers of soldiers go into service with smartphones in their vest pockets, the "storeroom" model of secrecy management is no longer viable (if, indeed, it ever was). Today, in the age of normalized digital militarism, public secrets seem to be in decline.

At first blush, these viral processes might seem a victory for crit-ics of Israel's military occupation. Today, social media pundits reassure us, little can be hidden from view. Today, Israeli society has to live with abundant online evidence of soldier indecency, of daily Israeli humili-ations of Palestinians, of routine disregard for Palestinian humanity, as

Today I visited a tunnel dug from #Gaza to #Israel by #Hamas for one purpose, #Terror. Check out my #Selfie http://t.co/2W2zLLC506

FIGURE 5.12.   SELFIE AS MILITARY INSTRUMENT, TWITTER, 2014. Selfie taken by Israeli military spokesman Lt. Col. Peter Lerner in Hamas tunnels during the 2014 Israeli bombardment of the Gaza Strip. SOURCE: https://twitter.com/LTCPeterLerner

images of its occupation violence and its Palestinian victims proliferate within the digital sphere in ways that Israelis cannot contain. Today, digital archives are telling it all in graphic detail.[32]

Or so it may seem. But in fact, some public secrets, some national ideologies, are remarkably recalcitrant, producing outcomes that run counter to techno-utopian investments in the political effects of digital proliferation and exposure. Consider, again, the mass selfie protests in support of a lone Israeli soldier. They shared an iconography with their selfie predecessors—weapons, ammunition, nudity—but with a difference. In most of these mobile snapshots, soldiers' faces were concealed. They aimed to avoid official retribution by the military, as Israeli pundits would explain, but anonymization also had a powerful symbolic valence.[33] Stripped of their faces, their individuality vanished, replaced by the national collective: "*We are all* David the Nahalite." These mass memes had, then, a dual relationship to the public secret, placing secrecy in something of a double bind. On the one hand, selfie protesters had embraced the scene of military violence against an unarmed Palestinian by identifying with the perpetrator. In this move, the violence of Israel's military occupation, and everyday Israeli complicity with its workings, was seemingly laid bare. In the process, the public secret was unsettled. But in replacing the individual with the collective, the face of the soldier with that of nation, personal responsibility and complicity disappeared: as such, the secret was consolidated again.

This double logic of secrecy, simultaneous breakdown and consolidation, resonates with broader tensions in the spheres of digital militarism today. As soldiers routinely carry smartphones into battle alongside their weaponry, as Israeli civilians joyfully produce and consume selfie militarism, as images of Israeli military brutality spread virally on Israeli and global social networks, the Israeli occupation becomes at once increasingly exposed and increasingly obscured. Now, private army snapshots from the field of military operations are migrating to Israeli Instagram accounts and Facebook albums, bringing the occupied West Bank into the heart of the Israeli metropolis in new ways. At the same time, the coupling of occupation and everyday digital conventions is working to banalize this violence, normalizing it through the veneer of the social media everyday, by which military rule is refigured as meme.

through social media: occupation is at once increasingly exposed and increasingly obscured

In our rendering, this normalized sphere of digital militarism, with its oscillating secrets, does not signal the occupation's immanent disappearance. Rather, it marks a collective Israeli embrace of its continuous enduring presence—less its history, than its future.

Afterword
#Revenge

"Hating Arabs isn't racism, it's values!" #IsraelDemandsRevenge
Israeli selfie, July 2014[1]

"#Revenge is the new feel-good summer hit in the Middle East."
Haaretz, July 2014[2]

IN THE SUMMER OF 2014, as this book moved into production, we watched the devastating Israeli bombardment of the Gaza Strip unfold in real time on our social media feeds. As Israeli bombs fell, as Palestinian civilian fatalities mounted, Palestinian journalists and residents from Gaza provided a constant stream of updates from the ground—video clips of the bombings, photographs of their destroyed homes, bloody images of children dying in hospitals, personal testimonies of terror and rage. Among global media pundits and anti-occupation activists bearing witness from afar, there was a sense that Palestinian wartime suffering and testimonials, easily accessible on our mobile screens, had never been more immediate.[3] Many Gazans invested considerable hope in this new digital reality—wondering if perhaps this time viral witnessing from Palestine might catalyze real political change.[4]

A very different social media field was unfolding concurrently in Israel, where digital militarism was being performed at unprecedented scales and degrees. During the course of the Gaza offensive, calls for violent attacks on Palestinians and Israeli leftists proliferated on Israeli social networks. The Israeli police and Justice Ministry reported growing "crimes of incitement" on social media, resulting in a dedicated "incitement hotline" to handle their volume.[5] Jewish Israeli users swapped detailed instructions on reporting "anti-Israeli" Facebook pages; Israeli journalists offered advice to parents ("Online Incitement: It's Up to the Parents," in the words of one headline); many mulled the question of whether "employees [should] get fired because of Facebook." Their answers varied considerably depending on the identity of the user: while most Israeli Jews were merely disciplined for hate speech, condemnation of the military operation by Israel's Palestinian citizens often ended in employment termination or institutional retribution at universities.[6]

Digital militarism had been growing in the weeks leading up to the Israeli offensive—particularly so following the abduction and killing of three Israeli settler teens by Palestinians from the West Bank, actions that catalyzed the Israeli bombardment (or, as some argued, had been used as its pretense). In response, as some Jewish Israeli extremist mobs roamed Israel's streets hunting Palestinian victims, others turned to Facebook to call for vengeance: "The People of Israel Demand Revenge."[7] The page quickly went viral, with thirty-four thousand "likes" in the day after its launch. Israeli fans voiced their support in the language of the selfie, uploading self-portraits with handmade placards demanding retribution (Figures A.1–A.3). Aside from the placards and the companion hashtag

FIGURE A.1. REVENGE SELFIE I, FACEBOOK, 2014. Israeli selfie campaign calling for violent retribution against Palestinians. Handwritten text on body reads, "The people of Israel demand revenge" (in Hebrew). SOURCE: https://www.facebook.com/AmIsraelDoreshNekama

(#IsraelDemandsRevenge), most of these selfies made no reference to violence. Their content was ordinary: a man in his living room surrounded
by children's toys; smiling teenage girls, their heads touching in a gesture
of friendship; a dog with puppies nested on an armchair. The signs were
equally commonplace, written on Post-It notes or pages torn from school
notebooks. As such, these selfies exemplified a central dynamic of digital
militarism: its interplay of violence and ordinary intimacy.

The object of #revenge was not specified on Facebook, but everyone
knew the implied target: "Death to the Arabs," "Death to every terrorist"—
slogans that would be repeated in political demonstrations, on radio talk
shows, and in Internet comments in the heated days that followed. These
slogans have a long history, popular among settler extremists during times
of perceived political or military threat. But they proliferated in the wake of
the 2014 kidnapping, as ideologies once relegated to Israel's social peripher-
ies were embraced by those in the mainstream, spreading virally through social networking. Some Israelis heeded the call in a very literal sense: the day
the Facebook page went live, Israeli police discovered the burned body of a
Palestinian teen, the victim of an Israeli revenge killing.[8] "This is a wake-up

FIGURE A.2. REVENGE SELFIE II, FACEBOOK, 2014. Post-it note reads, "Bibi, the
people of Israel demand revenge" (in Hebrew). SOURCE: https://www.facebook.com/
AmIsraelDoreshNekama

FIGURE A.3. REVENGE SELFIE III, FACEBOOK, 2014. Poster reads, "Hating Arabs isn't racism, it's values!" (in Hebrew). SOURCE: https://www.facebook.com/AmIsraelDoreshNekama

call," said a few Israeli voices from the left. "A line has been crossed."[9] But the violence would only grow, moving into state hands. In the week that followed, the Israeli military bombardment of the Gaza Strip would begin.

In some sense, the digital militarism that unfolded during the course of the military incursion took rather predictable forms, albeit at greater scales and degrees: the patriotic mobilization, the military propaganda efforts, the racist tweets and posts, the beautified soldier selfies, the joyful celebration of Palestinian deaths, the discourse of digital suspicion.[10] All epitomized developments of the two decades prior, a period that had culminated in the gradual normalization of digital militarism. And yet, the digital militarism of this period went one step further. Recall the viral selfie campaign in support of an aggressive Israeli soldier ("We are all with David the Nahalite"), explored in Chapter 5. Here, selfie solidarity had stood at something of a distance from soldier violence; such is the nature of solidarity, standing *with* but not *as* the violent aggressor. The #revenge campaign had narrowed this distance. As Israelis called for vengeance from their own social media accounts, they acted as aggressive agents in their own right by collectively demanding violent retribution.

Israeli digital militarism has long promoted state violence against Palestinians. Yet extremist violence—namely, calls for the killing of Palestinians—has been largely confined to the social media margins or staged in euphemistic terms. In 2014, the Israeli dream of killing moved out of the social media's shadows. In the process, the time of digital militarism shifted. Recall the 2013 Israeli sniper on Instagram with his mobile snapshot of the Palestinian boy in crosshairs. The violence portrayed is harsh and uncompromising, but its time is less than certain. Is the boy about to be shot? Was he merely photographed but never killed? Or was he already dead, killed at the time of the image's viral circulation?[11] As these varied readings suggest, the image is ambiguous in this regard. Indeed, it could be argued that its sadistic force lies precisely in the boy's capacity to die in multiple times: past, present, and future. The #revenge selfies, by contrast, call for violence in unequivocal terms and times. Here, Israelis were demanding immediate retribution, summoning reprisal attacks against Palestinians, now and in the future. And tragically, with the Gaza offensive, the state would comply.

We are identifying a shift in digital militarism that runs parallel to its normalization: from killing in an ambiguous time to blunt calls for deadly futures. This shift raises larger questions about the temporal terms of digital militarism throughout the years of its development and consolidation. As we have suggested, time has played a substantial role within the Israeli networked relationship to its military occupation, an integral component of maintaining public secrecy. The most prevalent temporality has been that of the present. It took shape within the recurrent narrative of "first times" that unfolded virally during the 2012 Gaza incursion (for example, "the first social media war"). It appeared in the narrative of social media "scandal" involving members of the Israeli armed forces, a storyline predicated on the fiction of a military breach without historical precedent, that unfolded *only now*. This recurrent discourse was bolstered by the time of the digital itself, both real and imagined: the live feed, the instantaneous share, the feverish pace of updates. In part, then, the presentism of digital militarism was the result of a category mistake, a blurring of medium and message: as if the time of the digital was the time of military occupation itself.

As a political tool, the discourse of presentism has a considerable history that exceeds both the Israel-Palestine context and the digital moment. As postcolonial scholars have documented, the fictive present tense was a central tenet of colonial ideologies. The story of "first contact," for example, was employed to narrate the non-West's encounter with Western modernity *for the very first time*, a break from the asynchronous time of pre-modernity—a narrative that naturalized colonialism through a "denial of coevalness."[12] The presentism of digital militarism rests on similar logic, rooted in similar disavowals of history, power, and violence. This static time has worked to obscure the occupation's long history; Israel's colonial and broader military histories recede beneath the weight of the absolute present, cleansing Israelis from a long history of culpability. In the process, the public secret is preserved.[13]

In the Israeli case, this temporal ideology was also reinforced by the national discourse of perpetual war: the notion of the constant state of siege, the existential threat. This ideology undergirds military policy and everyday Israeli practices alike: always be on alert, take note of suspicious persons, watch for the package at your feet.[14] The perpetual war coexists with the specter of the *future war*—that imprecise but certain future in which Israelis are schooled: always anticipate the next battle, a regional conflict that may erupt at any time; an incursion into the Gaza Strip is always eminent. For many Israelis, this future seems to have been already secured, even if its precise coordinates cannot be anticipated. For many, this future has the status of a normalized inevitability.

The future was on many Israeli minds in the aftermath of the 2014 Gaza bombardment. In the weeks prior, Israelis had called for deadly Palestinian futures, as we have argued. But in the aftermath of the military offensive, many began speaking about Israeli futures, and often in urgent and anxious tones. "More than ever," wrote one Israeli journalist as the incursion wound to a close, "Israel has accepted that it is locked in a game stacked against it . . . [that] a political solution is impossible."[15] In a similar vein, others mourned the unraveling of the Zionist dream, a dystopian lament about vanishing national horizons: "If our society is unable to . . . remove some of the settlements, that will signal that the Israeli story is finished, that the story of Zionism as we understand it, as I understand it, is over."[16] Many agreed that in this political moment, any sense of futurity was inconceivable: "Here in this place, tomorrow refuses to come. Every day, I feel anew as if we are reliving yesterday. We, as an Israeli and Palestinian collective, cling tightly to this nightmarish yesterday of injustice and revenge, and refuse to let go until we have finished autopsying its rotten corpse."[17]

Two different visions of the future were emerging together. Israelis were calling for deadly Palestinian futures and supporting the state's bloody campaign in Gaza, even as they were lamenting their own missing future. A familiar transposition was thus at work: even amidst devastating Israeli state violence with its disproportionate toll on Palestinian lives, Israelis were representing themselves as the occupation's chief victim. In 2014, as calls for #revenge went viral, this familiar storyline took on a new tenor. Perhaps the no-future to which so many Israelis were gesturing was an Israel without its public secrets—that is, the impossible prospect of living intimately with Israeli state violence without a disavowal of complicity.

. . .

We began this book by framing it as an archival project. And it is here we conclude. For we believe that when read as an archive, this material may offer some alternatives in these difficult political times.

But what kind of archive is this? In the broadest terms, it is a perpetrators' archive, a chronicle of self-documented Israeli racism and militarism on social media, a digital record of living in intimate complicity with Israel's military rule, in both living rooms and battlefields. It is also a chronicle of the shifting terms of public secrecy management in the social media age, a record of the new digital tactics by which Israelis are laboring to contain the spillover of state violence into the Israeli civilian everyday. Today, as this book has shown, acts of complicity and secrecy management have taken root in the commonplace terms of social media—in networking practices, protocols, grammar, and associated affect. They have been seamlessly enfolded into the fabric of ordinary Israeli digital life.

As scholars of new media remind us, digital archives are by no means static.[18] Rather, they shift and mutate alongside developments in database technologies and user archival practices. But despite such shifts, most objects housed in a digital archive (the tweets, Facebook posts, Instagram images, and so on) are not temporary—or not usually. They can remain on computer servers long after their producers and consumers have forgotten them—often even when deleted, made private by their posters, or professionally scrubbed by content moderators—buried under new layers of digital data. In this sense, despite their seemingly fleeting nature, many digital objects enjoy long afterlives that their creators can neither fully anticipate nor control. The digital archive, then, does not live in a single time. Its past and present are always enfolded within dormant digital futures.[19]

And here political possibilities lie. We want to propose that this archive, with its potential longevity and retrievability, might yield political alternatives in these difficult times—however uncertain, however utopian. In the digital archive, although redolent with past violence, Israeli militarism is rarely static. As such, it can unfold onto a set of histories, political processes, and structures of complicity that militant Israeli communities have tried to obscure. With its multiple afterlives, it might function as an important political counterweight, working against Israeli legacies of forgetting and erasure that have protected the public secret. Viewed in this way, the digital archive of militarism and occupation opens the possibility for Israeli accountability. Perhaps, in the process, a different future becomes imaginable.

Reference Matter

Acknowledgments

We met at an academic conference in 2009 when, in the aftermath of Israel's bloody incursion into the Gaza Strip of that year (2008–2009), we were each trying to understand how new media and communication technologies were changing Israel's political playing field, its military occupation, and its relationship to the larger Middle East. Our collaboration grew and developed alongside the development of Israeli digital militarism itself. Perhaps ironically, our work would not have been possible without new digital communication technologies themselves—chiefly a Skype connection that, although often spotty and unstable, allowed us to write jointly across continents and time zones.

We are enormously grateful to the numerous friends, colleagues, and interlocutors who generously provided materials, feedback, and critical engagement with earlier drafts and essays: Miriyam Aouraugh, Joel Beinin, Lauren Berlant, Alex Fattal, Debra Ferreday, Dana Golan, Neve Gordon, Hannah Green, Jeff Green, Judith Green, Omri Grinberg, Richard Grinker, Zeynep Gursel, Caren Kaplan, Sarah Kendzior, Laleh Khalili, Ronit Lentin, Melani McAlister, Alejandro Paz, Silvia Posocco, Ruth Preser, Shira Robinson, Sima Shakhsari, Yehuda Shaul, Noam Sheizaf, Ted Swedenburg, Helga Tawil-Souri, Chris Toensing, Janine Zacharia, and colleagues with *Shovrim Shtika*, Breaking the Silence. Special thanks to all those who went above and beyond, supporting us throughout the writing process. Richard Stein, Rebecca's father, was our most tireless and insightful reader during the manuscript's many stages, generously ushering the book into its final form. This book bears the marks of his sharp eyes throughout. Adi thanks Yehudit Kirstein-Keshet for offering poignant insights, Adi Moreno for assistance with numerous online examples, and Kelly Nip for helping to sustain work-life balance. Rebecca thanks Sarah Abrevaya Stein for unfailing encouragement; Negar Mottahedeh, whose astute engagements helped seed this project; and Omri Grinberg for countless hours gathering and analyzing digital texts.

Sharing our ideas in seminars, conferences, and workshops was crucial as the book evolved. Together, we shared an earlier draft of our introduction at "Social Media and Political Horizons: Israel/Palestine, the Middle East and Beyond" at the University of Manchester. We are grateful to Moshe Behar, Simon Faulkner, Yasmin Ibrahim, Theresa Senft, Anastasia Valassopoulos, and Farida Vis, who offered a dedicated reading during the conference and workshop, and in subsequent email exchanges. Thanks to Duke's Department of Jewish Studies for their generous funding of this event. Adi thanks audiences at the Jewish Studies Seminar Series at the University of Manchester (U.K.), the Media Studies Seminar at Hull University (U.K.), Citizen Media Colloquium (Manchester, U.K.), *iRhetoric in Russian* conference (Passau, Germany), Digital Emotions network and launch (Amsterdam, Holland), and the Media Studies seminar at Ben-Gurion University (Israel), as well as her students in courses on Internet ethnographies and research methods for their suggestions. Rebecca thanks audiences at the University of California, Berkeley, Department of Anthropology; University of California, Los Angeles, Middle East Studies; University of California, Davis, American Studies; California State University, Long Beach, Department of History; Johns Hopkins University, Department of Anthropology; Stanford University, Modern Thought and Literature Program; McMaster University, Jewish Studies; McGill University, Department of Anthropology; Yale University, American Studies; Duke University, "*Occupations*, Concept Workshop," Birzeit University, Department of Media. Rebecca thanks her graduate students—particularly Yaekin Abdelmagid, Anna Dowell, Alyssa Miller, Andrea Patino, and Louis Yako—for dialogues along the way, and students in "The Cultures of New Media" for insights that only digital natives possess. Earlier versions of our analysis appeared in *Middle East Report*, *Critical Inquiry* blog, and *London Review of Books* blog. We thank these publications for the opportunity to first develop these ideas in their pages.

Dedicated research assistants in Israel and North America performed skillful sleuthing. Rebecca thanks Shira Makin, Starlyn Matheny, Itamar Radai, and Ido Ramati. Thanks also to Nir Schnaiderman for plentiful assistance. At Duke, librarians Linda Daniels and Ciara Healy provided consistent support. We wholeheartedly thank Tyler Atkins for unstinting hard work and sharp eyes, Jim Henderson for indexing work, and Mariana Raykov at Stanford University Press for patiently ushering the book into production. Kate Wahl, our editor, consistently went above and beyond her editorial duties to encourage us and support our emerging volume. We also thank anonymous reviewers for Stanford University Press for useful critique and suggestions.

Rebecca's initial research was supported by several grants from foundations and institutes: the Wenner-Gren Foundation, the Palestinian American Research

Center (PARC), the Josiah Charles Trent Memorial Foundation Endowment Fund. Adi's initial research was supported by the Leverhulme Trust (U.K.) and the Simon Research Fellowship, the University of Manchester (U.K.). Thanks also to the Carnegie Corporation of New York, Duke Jewish Studies, and Manchester University Simon Research Fund for generous assistance with book subvention and scholarly workshops that led to the volume's development. The statements made and views expressed in this book are solely our own.

Last, we are indebted to our families, who patiently endured the challenges that collaborative, cross-continent work brings. Adi: thank you, MHK, for your generous patience and being my anchor. Rebecca: thank you Andrew, my partner in all things, for never faltering; Isaac and Saul for your curiosity. Thank you all for being there, for supporting us, and reminding us what really matters.

Notes

Preface

1. Morozov, *Net Delusion*.
2. We discuss the literature on Israel's occupation in Chapter 1; see note 11, p. 106.
3. Gitelman, *Always Already New*.

Chapter 1

1. Netanyahu made this comment during a keynote address to the CyberTech 2014 Conference, Tel Aviv, on January 28, 2014. The speech can be viewed at "PM Netanyahu's Keynote Speech at CyberTech 2014 Conference, 2014."
2. Israeli Ministry of Tourism, "Communications in Israel."
3. Mehmood, "'Israel Is Addicted to Occupation'—Gideon Levy."
4. This was the first war in which Israeli soldiers deployed in large numbers with smartphones. We discuss the history of soldier mobile and smartphone usage, and military policy governing this usage, in Chapter 2. In 2014, the Israeli military unveiled new plans for "military grade" encrypted smartphones for soldier use. See Ziv, "Israel's Defense Ministry Signs Deal for Military-Grade Smartphones."
5. Peled, "The First Social Media War Between Israel and Gaza."
6. The *Oxford English Dictionary* defines *selfie* as "A photographic self-portrait; *esp.* one taken with a smartphone or webcam and shared via social media" ("Selfie, N."). However, there is considerable disagreement among scholars regarding the parameters of the selfie genre. In our rendering, we include portraits taken by others but shared by the subject in question on their social networks. The growing popularity in Israel of so-called selfie sticks, enabling mobile self-portraiture from arm's length, has further complicated the genre. We discuss Israeli soldier selfies in Chapter 5. This particular Instagram archive can be found at Notopoulos, "Surreal Instagrams from Israel Defense Forces Soldiers." For discussion of the broader history and use of cameras by soldiers within larger geopolitical contexts, see Struk, *Private Pictures*.

7. According to 2013 public statements from the Israel military, this Instagram archive was in violation of the army's emerging social media policy; historically, this policy has been rarely enforced. For a recent articulation of such policy as it pertains to Facebook, see Cohen, "A New Directive Will Impose Restrictions IDF Soldiers' Use of Facebook."

8. For further discussion of iconographies of Israeli soldiering, see Brownfield-Stein, *Fantasy of the State*; Brownfield-Stein, "Visual Representations of IDF Women Soldiers and 'Civil-Militarism' in Israel"; and Yosef, *Beyond Flesh*. On the longer legacy of Israeli soldiering as a project of self-making, see Sasson-Levy, "Individual Bodies, Collective State Interests."

9. The me-centered character of such mobile self-portrait images is part of the broader trend of micro-celebrity and self-branding that increasingly characterizes social media usage among young people. See Senft, "Microcelebrity and the Branded Self." For an excellent analysis of the Israeli military's embrace of branding culture, see Lemmey, "Devastation in Meatspace."

10. The U.S. blogger responsible for the widespread circulation of these images would call them "surreal." Notopoulos, "Surreal Instagrams from Defense Forces Soldiers."

11. Our analysis is informed by recent and foundational scholarship on the Israeli military occupation, particularly scholarship attentive to the role of cultural technologies, discursive formations, and modes of governmentality in the workings of military rule. See, for example, Azoulay and Ophir, *The One-State Condition*; Gordon, *Israel's Occupation*; Weizman, *Hollow Land*; and Weizman, *The Least of All Possible Evils*. We also draw on literature on the interplay between militarism and the entertainment industry and on the mediated aesthetics of war. New and foundational writings include Azoulay, *The Civil Contract of Photography*; Derian, *Virtuous War;* Dyer-Witheford and De Peuter, *Games of Empire*; Mirzoeff, *Watching Babylon*; Morris, *Believing Is Seeing*; Stahl, *Militainment, Inc.*; and Virilio, *War and Cinema*. For a fuller genealogy of the existing scholarship on Israeli militarism, see note 37, p. 110.

12. We borrow the phrase "networked publics," which we employ throughout this book, from social media scholar danah boyd. She defines it thusly: "Networked publics are publics that are restructured by networked technologies. As such, they are simultaneously (1) the space constructed through networked technologies and (2) the imagined community that emerges as a result of the intersection of people, technology and practice." boyd, *It's Complicated*, 8. For a broader discussion of Internet cultures and digital communications in Israel, including the use of such tools by the Israeli left activist community, see Ashuri, "(Web)sites of Memory and the Rise of Moral Mnemonic Agents"; Doron and

Lev-On, *New Media, Politics and Society in Israel*; Hijazi-Omari and Ribak, "Playing with Fire"; and Schejter and Tirosh, "Social Media New and Old in the Al-'Arakeeb Conflict." During the years chronicled in this book, the Israeli left, veterans of Internet use for political ends, relied heavily on social media, their ability to self-publish providing a means by which to circumvent the constrained ideological terms of the national media, with social media increasingly functioning as a counter-archive of the military occupation.

13. Karatzogianni, *The Politics of Cyberconflict*; Karatzogianni, "Introduction"; Kozaryn, "Tactical Internet Key to Digital Battlefield."

14. Recent scholarly research on the militarization of social media includes Alper, "War on Instagram"; Chancey, "New Media"; Hjorth and Pink, "New Visualities and the Digital Wayfarer"; Kaplan, "The Biopolitics of Technoculture in the Mumbai Attacks"; Lawson, "The US Military's Social Media Civil War"; Lynch, Freelon, and Aday, *Syria's Socially Mediated Civil War*; Morozov, *The Net Delusion*; Pötzsch, "The Emergence of iWar"; and Susca, "Why We Still Fight." Recent popular writings on this topic are also extensive, including Berkman, "Russia Blocks Pro-Ukraine Groups on Social Media"; Gregory, "Inside Putin's Campaign of Social Media Trolling and Faked Ukrainian Crimes"; "How Researchers Use Social Media to Map the Conflict in Syria"; Kantrowitz, "The United States' Social Media Plan to Keep Syria's Chemical Weapons Safe"; and McBain, "In Syria, the Internet Has Become Just Another Battleground"; "Military Announces New Social Media Policy"; "The Role of Social Media in the Syrian Civil War."

15. This book does not address the use of digital media by Palestinians in the West Bank, the Gaza Strip, Israel, or the Palestinian Diaspora, although our work is informed by scholarship on these matters. See, for example, Abu-Zayyad, "Human Rights, the Internet and Social Media"; Aouragh, "Confined Offline"; Aouragh, *Palestine Online*; Aouragh, "Virtual Intifada"; Asthana and Havandjian, "Youth Media Imaginaries in Palestine"; Cook, "Palestinian Social Media Campaigns Unlike Egyptian, Tunisian Counterparts"; Junka-Aikio, "Late Modern Subjects of Colonial Occupation"; Khalili, "Virtual Nation"; Sienkiewicz, "Out of Control"; and Tawil-Souri, "Digital Occupation." For a broader discussion of Internet culture in the context of the Arab Israeli conflict, see Marmura, *Hegemony in the Digital Age*; Sucharov and Sasley, "Blogging Identities on Israel/Palestine"; and Alsaafin, "Palestinians Turn to Facebook in Fight Against Occupation." On the state of the Palestinian ITC sector in general, see Alsaafin, "Palestinians Turn to Facebook in Fight Against Occupation"; Musleh, "Maath Musleh on Social Media and Palestine"; *Palestinian Central Bureau of Statistics (PCBS) Reviews the Current Use of Technology in the Palestin-*

ian Territory on the Occasion of World Information Society Day; and *Palestinian ICT Sector 2.0.*

16. On militarism by other means, see Clough, "War by Other Means."

17. For example, Israel has long had large per-capita mobile phone adoption. In 2009, 91.8 percent of Israeli households possessed mobile phones. Central Bureau of Statistics, quoted in Schejter and Cohen, "Mobile Phone Usage as an Indicator of Solidarity." In 2013, Israel was said to lead Europe and the United States in smartphone use; see Hoffman, "57% of Israelis Have Smartphones," and Schejter and Cohen, "Mobile Phone Usage as an Indicator of Solidarity." For a study of the role of mobile phones within Israeli national culture, see Cohen, Lemish, and Schejter, *The Wonder Phone in the Land of Miracles.*

18. Russell, "Israelis Are Now the World's Biggest Social Network Addicts, Says New Report."

19. Acar, "Culture, Corruption, Suicide, Happiness and Global Social Media Use." Recent statistics on Israeli social media usage can be found at Fiske, "Israelis Love Their Touch Screens"; "Israel Ranks 7 in Global Broadband Penetration"; "The World Bank DataBank: Israel"; and Economist Intelligence Unit, *Digital Economy Rankings 2010.*

20. Many high-tech startups in Israel have been incubated in military environments or for Israeli military purposes. For discussion of linkages between the Israeli military and the high-tech sector, see Gordon, "Israel's Emergence as a Homeland Security Capital"; Gordon, *The Political Economy of Israel's Homeland Security Industry*; and Swed and Butler, "Military Capital in the Israeli Hi-Tech Industry."

21. The phrase "Start Up Nation" is the title of this celebrated volume about Israel: Senor, Council on Foreign Relations, and Singer, *Start-up Nation.* The notion of "high-tech Zionism" was articulated by net artist and media designer Tsila Hassine, interview by Rebecca L. Stein, May 2013. For broader discussion of such issues, see Latham, *Bombs and Bandwidth.*

22. Israeli commentator Noam Sheizaf, writing in 2014, has proposed that Israel is a "country whose politics had been dominated by the conflict for a century." See Sheizaf, "Film Review." On this use of this euphemistic slang by Israeli citizens, see Steinberg, "The 'Matzav,'" and Brumer, "Conversations."

23. On growing disinterest in the so-called peace process, see Levy, "Israel Does Not Want Peace."

24. This cartographic fiction was anticipated in the 1992 political slogan of the Israeli Labor party, which framed Israel's ideal relationship to the Palestinians this way: "Us here, them there." Blecher, "Living on the Edge."

25. For a discussion of the prevailing Israeli fiction that Gaza is not occupied,

see Derfner, "Ceasefire Tells the World," and Hajjar, "Is Gaza Still Occupied and Why Does It Matter?" According to the United Nations, the Gaza Strip remains occupied—an argument with which Israelis are in fierce opposition. See Neuer, "Hamas Says Gaza 'Not Occupied'; UN Disagrees," and Samson, "Is Gaza Occupied?" For a review of the legal debates on this issue, see Darcy and Reynolds, "'Otherwise Occupied.'"

26. For discussion of the Israeli 2011 summer protests, particularly their sidelining of questions of military occupation, see Grinberg, "The J14 Resistance Mo(ve)ment," and Monterescu and Shaindlinger, "Situational Radicalism."

27. See Levinson and Zarchin, "Netanyahu-Appointed Panel," and Sheizaf, "Panel Appointed by Netanyahu Concludes: There Is No Occupation."

28. Matar, "Bit by Bit, Coverage of Occupation Disappears from Israeli News."

29. For an example of *occupation* in question marks, see "Israeli-Arab Party Blames 'Occupation' for Violence After Kidnapped Teens Found Dead." For a corrective to such fictions, written by the former head of the Israeli human rights organization B'tselem and aimed at Israeli and Jewish American audiences, see "Op-Ed: The West Bank Is Under Military Occupation, and That's a Fact."

30. For background on the West Bank settlement infrastructure, see "47 Years of Temporary Occupation."

31. For discussion of the Jewish Israeli public's rightward shift in the prior decade, see Beinin and Stein, "Histories and Futures of a Failed Peace."

32. Cook, "Cultures of Hate"; and Lapide, "'Jewish Nationalism' Behind Young Palestinian's Death—Asia News." See also Beinin, "Racism Is the Foundation of Israel's Operation Protective Edge," and Sokatch, "Not Only in Gaza."

33. There is a large literature advancing these propositions, including Aikins and Reddick, *Web 2.0 Technologies and Democratic Governance*; Akrivopoulou and Garipidis, *Digital Democracy and the Impact of Technology on Governance and Politics*; Anduiza, Jensen, and Jorba, *Digital Media and Political Engagement Worldwide*; Boler, *Digital Media and Democracy*; Diamond and Plattner, *Liberation Technology*; Dijk and Hacker, *Digital Democracy*; Gibson, Römmele, and Ward, *Electronic Democracy*; Hague and Loader, *Digital Democracy*; and Ziccardi, *Resistance, Liberation Technology and Human Rights in the Digital Age*.

34. Works that advance a digital democracy paradigm in the context of the 2011 Arab revolts include Howard and Hussain, *Democracy's Fourth Wave?* and el-Nawawy and Khamis, *Egyptian Revolution 2.0*. In recent years, many scholars have also critiqued this proposition, but chiefly for its failure to consider the interplay between economic power and the digital world. Such critiques include Hindman, *The Myth of Digital Democracy*, and McChesney, *Digital Disconnect*.

There is also a growing scholarship reassessing the role of digital media in Middle East political theaters more generally. See Downey, *Uncommon Grounds*.

35. This corrective is most famously advanced by Evgeny Morozov. Morozov, *The Net Delusion*; also see Aouragh, "Framing the Internet in the Arab Revolutions," and Hindman, *The Myth of Digital Democracy*.

36. Karatzogianni, *The Politics of Cyberconflict* and "Introduction."

37. Scholars identify several key historical junctures in the legacy of Israeli militarism. These include the early days of Zionist settlement in Palestine, from its emergence during the pre- (*Yishuv*) and early years of state formation when the ethos of a "nation in arms" was shaped and the military solution to the so-called "Arab-Israeli conflict" was first legitimized; through the impact of Nazi fascism and the Holocaust on Israeli national identity, state policy, and popular discourses of security; through the shifts in the state's security policy and popular Israeli perceptions of national identity that attended the onset of the 1967 occupation; through the swell of national protest and harsh critique of state actions that followed the 1982 Israeli war on Lebanon; through waves of Palestinian resistance in the occupied territories (chiefly, the first and second *Intifadas*); through the ways a globalized "war on terror" was imported into the Israeli security paradigm; to the declining Jewish youth investment in either Zionism or army service, a position articulated chiefly through lifestyle rather than politics. For a discussion of these and other foundational junctures and trends within the history of Israeli militarism, see Barak and Sheffer, *Militarism and Israeli Society*; Ben-Ari, *Mastering Soldiers*; Ben-Eliezer, *The Making of Israeli Militarism*; Kanaaneh, *Surrounded*; Kimmerling, *The Invention and Decline of Israeliness*; Lomsky-Feder and Ben-Ari, *The Military and Militarism in Israeli Society*; and Maman and Ben-Ari, *Military, State, and Society in Israel*.

38. On gender, see Sasson-Levy, "From the Military as a Gendered Organization to Militarized Inequality Regimes," and Sasson-Levy, *Identities in Uniform*. On queer sexualities, see Kaplan, *Brothers and Others in Arms*; Kuntsman, "The Soldier and the Terrorist"; and Stein, "EXPLOSIVE Scenes from Israel's Gay Occupation." On reproduction, see Ivry, *Embodying Culture*. On Israeli childhood, see Golden, "Childhood as Protected Space?," and Golden, "Fear, Politics and Children." On education, see Gor, "Education for War in Israel." On art and culture, see Harris and Omer-Sherman, *Narratives of Dissent*, and Yosef, *Beyond Flesh*. On consumer practices, see Stein, *Itineraries in Conflict*. Our analysis is also informed by the work of the Israeli feminist NGO New Profile: The Movement for the Demilitarization of Israeli Society. For information on the organization, see their institutional webpage: "New Profile: The Movement to Demilitarize Israeli Society."

39. Kimmerling, "Militarism in Israeli Society," and Kimmerling, *The Invention and Decline of Israeliness.*

40. Kimmerling, *The Invention and Decline of Israeliness*, 11.

41. Stewart, *Ordinary Affects.*

42. "Holy Instagram. War becomes hip, social & sexy thanks 2 the IDF"; "Israeli soldiers on instagram, posing and having fun. Murder is funny to them apparently." These and other responses from social media users can be found at O'Neil, "Israeli Soldiers Shock the Web with Smiling Instagram Photos." Some pundits argued that these perverse images were evidence that Israel was losing its social media war. See Eördögh, "Instagram Photos of Smiling Soldiers Show Israel Is Now Losing Its Gaza Social Media War."

43. On algorithms and hashtag politics in the Israel/Palestine context, see Vis, "Collecting Data for #pillarofdefense and #failing."

44. For discussion of haunted futurities, see Ferreday and Kuntsman, "Introduction: Haunted Futures."

45. We thank Helga Tawil Souri for pushing us to elaborate our theory of time; we continue this discussion in the Afterword. On the normalization of war in the Israeli context, see Ben-Ari and Lomsky-Feder, "The Discourses of 'Psychology' and the 'Normalization' of War in the Israeli Context"; Gavriely-Nuri, *The Normalization of War in Israeli Discourse, 1967–2008*; and Shefer, *Militarism and Israeli Society.*

46. Taussig, *Defacement.* For additional scholarly discussions of the "public" or "open" secret and linkages between secrecy and security, see Masco, "'Sensitive but Unclassified'"; Masco, *The Theater of Operations*; Miller, "Secret Subjects, Open Secrets"; and Sedgwick, *Epistemology of the Closet.*

47. Azoulay and Ophir, *The One-State Condition.*

48. Today, some Israeli anti-occupation activists use the language of secrecy to describe this condition, this collective failure to contend with the realities of Israeli military rule: "The story of IDF service . . . has been erased from [Israeli] public life and mired in *secrecy*, with soldiers largely choosing to keep their families, communities and the entire Israeli society in the dark about what they have to do in order to maintain military occupation over another people." Breaking the Silence email newsletter, May 23, 2014; emphasis ours.

49. This has been the case when Israel's collective grappling with the history of the Nakba is concerned. Although this history was largely invisible within the political imaginary of the Israeli left during the 1980s and early 1990s, it would gradually come into visibility over the course of the next decade, led by the Israeli activist group Zochrot. For greater discussion, see Stein, "Israeli Routes Through Nakba Landscapes."

Chapter 2

1. Maj. Avital Leibovich, the former head of the Israeli Defense Forces' foreign press branch; 2008. Originally published in *The Jerusalem Post*. Quoted in Hodge, "YouTube, Twitter: Weapons in Israel's Info War."

2. Ronen, "IDF's Cyber-Commander Prepares Internet Assault."

3. "The Truth About the Middle East."

4. "Israel to Pay Students to Defend It Online."

5. "Mowing the Lawn."

6. The tweet from @IDFSpokesman read, "The IDF has begun a widespread campaign on terror sites & operatives in the #Gaza Strip, chief among them #Hamas & Islamic Jihad targets." @IDFSpokesman, Twitter post.

7. "Only Israel can sell a massacre like they're promoting a movie. They take war crimes and massacres to an art form." @Joseph_in_OC, Twitter post.

8. From @AlqassamBrigade: "@IDFspokesperson Our blessed hands will reach your leaders and soldiers wherever they are (You Opened Hell Gates on Yourselves)." @AlqassamBrigade, Twitter post.

9. Headlines to this effect filled the global mediasphere, such as "First Twitter War Declaration?" and "First Social Media War Between Israel and Gaza." See "First Twitter War Declaration? Israel Announces Gaza Operation on Social Media Site," and Peled, "The First Social Media War Between Israel and Gaza." One follower of the IDF Twitter feed responded, "The first war on Twitter has just begun."

10. Sutter, "Will Twitter War Become the New Norm?"

11. The Iranian revolution of 2009 was also celebrated by Western analysts as the first "Twitter Revolution." For a critique of this claim, see Morozov, *The Net Delusion*. See Silverstone, "What's New About New Media? Introduction" and Rayner, "The Novelty Trap," for analogous critiques of the novelty claims that attend "new media" studies and popular discourse.

12. For discussion of the history of the term "new media," see Lievouw, "Theorizing New Media."

13. Gitelman, *Always Already New*.

14. This chapter is based on our earlier study of this topic, one of the earliest to consider social media's role in the Israel-Palestine context from the vantage of the Israeli state and patriotic Israeli users. Kuntsman and Stein, "Another War Zone." Since the time of that writing, scholarship and journalistic accounts of this phenomenon have proliferated. Scholarly works on the topic include Allan and Brown, "The Mavi Marmara at the Frontlines of Web 2.0"; Archibald and Miller, "Full-Spectacle Dominance?"; Bennett, "Exploring the Impact of an Evolving War and Terror Blogosphere on Traditional Media Coverage of Conflict";

Berenger, *Cybermedia Go to War*; Berenger, *Social Media Go to War*; Carafano, *Wiki at War*; Fahmy and Eakin, "High Drama on the High Seas"; Heemsbergen and Lindgren, "The Power of Precision Air Strikes and Social Media Feeds in the 2012 Israel-Hamas Conflict"; Hoskins and O'Loughlin, *War and Media*; Mazumdar, "Shifting Blame on the High Seas . . . and on YouTube"; Sumiala and Tikka, "Broadcast Yourself"; and Ward, "Social Media in the Gaza Conflict."

15. All of these military actions were described as "wars" in mainstream Israeli state and media discourse. Many Israeli activists would argue that the language of "war" obfuscated the continuing Israeli military occupation by characterizing Israeli violence as a sudden eruption rather than the product of a long occupation history. On the politics of this nomenclature, see Azoulay, "Declaring the State of Israel."

16. For a further discussion of these events, see Karatzogianni, *The Politics of Cyberconflict*.

17. Abdel-Latif, "It's War—Virtually"; Al-Rizzo, "The Undeclared Cyberspace War Between Hezbollah and Israel"; Karatzogianni, *The Politics of Cyberconflict*.

18. Weimann, *Terror on the Internet*.

19. Al-Rizzo, "The Undeclared Cyberspace War Between Hezbollah and Israel"; Karatzogianni, *The Politics of Cyberconflict*. Leaders in the Internet sector decried "the current onslaught of cyberattacks against Israel's key websites" as "perhaps the most extensive, coordinated, malicious hacking effort in history." Cited in Allen and Demchak, "The Palestinian-Israeli Cyberwar."

20. Cited in Weimann, *Terror on the Internet*, 197.

21. Schwartz, "Hacker Defaces Pro-Israel Web Site as the Mideast Conflict Expands into Cyberspace."

22. Karatzogianni, *The Politics of Cyberconflict*, 156.

23. "IDF Broadcasts Hizbullah's Dead on Al-Manar"; Peri, "IDF Hacks Nasrallah's TV Channel."

24. Karatzogianni, *The Politics of Cyberconflict*, 157. Such exchanges also rendered the Internet a new domain of nonviolent resistance in which political dialogue was being refashioned in the technical language of competing hacker abilities.

25. Some scholars and activists would argue that this phenomenon, bent on advancing national political interests and demonstrating computer proficiency, had the paradoxical effect of connecting young people on opposite sides of the national and political frontline in a trend that some scholars have described as a "*dialogue* between hackers." Al-Rizzo, "The Undeclared Cyberspace War Between Hezbollah and Israel," 398. On the reframing of the political in hacker terms, see Karatzogianni, *The Politics of Cyberconflict*, 16–157, and Vacca, *Guide to Wireless Network Security*, 491–492.

26. Al-Rizzo, "The Undeclared Cyberspace War Between Hezbollah and Israel."

27. Saad, Bazan, and Varin, "Asymmetric Cyber-Warfare Between Israel and Hezbollah."

28. Weimann, *Terror on the Internet*.

29. Denning, "Information Technology and Security."

30. Caldwell, Menning, and Murphy, "Learning to Leverage New Media"; Kalb and Saivetz, "The Israeli-Hezbollah War of 2006."

31. Caldwell, Menning, and Murphy, "Learning to Leverage New Media"; Saad, Bazan, and Varin, "Asymmetric Cyber-Warfare Between Israel and Hezbollah."

32. In this and other chapters, we use the official names of Israel's military operations in order to signal the rhetorical norms of the army. This should not be read as an embrace of the military mind-set nor the ways nomenclature is used to sanitize state violence.

33. Gilinsky, "How Social Media War Was Waged in Gaza-Israel Conflict."

34. Activist populations had long been among Israel's most active and savvy social media users, a phenomenon made dramatically evident during the aftermath of the Flotilla affair of 2008. Their sizable presence on digital platforms far outstripped their marginal political import and scale within the nation-state.

35. Russian-speaking immigrants living in Israel used the network extensively at the time of the incursion, significantly expanding their earlier efforts of pro-Israeli mobilization during the second Lebanon War (2006). LiveJournal was the most popular blogging social network among Russian speakers worldwide at the time, both in Russia and in Russian-speaking émigré communities worldwide, including Israel. For a detailed discussion of their online activities, see Kuntsman, "Webs of Hate in Diasporic Cyberspaces."

36. These two blogger communities were called "The Gaza War Through Bloggers Eyes" and "Our Truth."

37. "Our Truth."

38. "Here we won't have any politics or debates between those on the Left or on the Right. . . . This military action [Cast Lead] is just, and is supported by all Zionist parties, beyond politics and elections." This post in LiveJournal, dated December 28, 2008, obscured the participation of left-wing Russian-Israeli bloggers in LiveJournal conversations.

39. See Caldwell, Menning, and Murphy, "Learning to Leverage New Media," and Kalb and Saivetz, "The Israeli-Hezbollah War of 2006."

40. For discussion of the media ban during Cast Lead, see Stein, "Impossible Witness."

41. "Israel Defense Forces."

42. This appeared in a video titled "Underground Weapons Storage Facility in Gaza Struck by Israel Air Force" (2009).

43. Many scholars have traced this mode of capturing war images to the American attacks on Iraq in 1991. See Sontag, *Regarding the Pain of Others*, and Azoulay, *The Civil Contract of Photography*. Some of the IDF's allegations about the contents of the YouTube visual field were subsequently disputed by human rights organizations who charged the military with image manipulation, and by YouTube viewers who briefly succeeded in removing some footage from public view, but these controversies did little to temper the initiative's popularity. The Israeli human rights group B'tselem took issue with the IDF's claims in the video "Rockets in Transit." See *Precisely Wrong: Gaza Civilians Killed by Israeli Drone-Launched Missiles*. Also see Al Jazeera's interview with B'tselem workers: *B'Tselem Questions Israeli Account of Attack*.

44. Byers, "Gaza: Secondary War Being Fought on the Internet"; Shachtman, "Israel's Accidental YouTube War."

45. In the early days of the incursion, Israeli officials also launched personal video blogs and delivered private briefings to international bloggers. The first video blog was uploaded to the IDF's dedicated YouTube channel on January 3, 2009: http://www.youtube.com/user/idfnadesk#p/c/24B346594DCE3F37/0/rfTr609 whl8. For one critique of such efforts, see Guarav, "War 2.0, Propaganda 2.0 or Public Diplomacy 2.0."

46. Twitter was a crucial platform for political engagement during this incursion. The hashtag #gaza ranked among the world's top ten tags throughout the war's duration—fueled, in part, by Al Jazeera's active Twitter feed from the Gaza Strip.

47. These critics charged the Israeli consulate with failing to understand popular Twitter conventions. For a sense of how such conventions are codified, see Boyd, Golder, and Lotan, "Tweet, Tweet, Retweet."

48. For a fuller discussion of the Israeli state's early foray into social media, see Stein, "StateTube." For a critique of such efforts, see Allan and Brown, "The Mavi Marmara at the Frontlines of Web 2.0." Popular media critiques included "How the IDF Fell Off the Social Media Bandwagon."

49. Shamir, "'Twitter Revolutionized Israeli Diplomacy.'" Most media pundits tended to agree: "We've seen governments try to control information on social media before," noted the blog editor at *The Guardian*, "but you haven't seen governments trying to use social media like this." Flintoff, "Gaza Conflict Plays Out Online Through Social Media."

50. This was a group of six ships organized by the "Free Gaza Movement"

and the Turkish Foundation for Human Rights and Freedoms and Humanitarian Relief.

51. For an overview of the social media wars that attended the Flotilla episodes, see Allan and Brown, "The Mavi Marmara at the Frontlines of Web 2.0." See also Sumiala and Tikka, "Broadcast Yourself."

52. The military attempted to stem activist media through confiscation of all onboard recording equipment and suspension of the convoy's live broadcasting stream, replacing it with official IDF information. Israeli military efforts at media blackout included blocking cell phone signals. On cell phone jamming, see Stelter, "Videos Carry On the Fight Over Sea Raid." On Israeli military efforts to control mobile networking and cell phone signals during the events in question, see Kuntsman and Stein, "Another War Zone."

53. Livestream is a live streaming video platform.

54. Facebook was a particularly vibrant locus of activist networking, with groups such as *Flotilla for Palestine* posting links to unfolding events and Twitter updates. Users also held web-based, flash-mob style protests, inviting supporters to alter their Facebook profile pictures with images of the siege or protest to reflect their solidarity. Others, such as "Jewish Voice for Peace" or "Israelis for Palestine," brought together Israelis and Jews outside Israel in opposition to the state's military tactics. Twitter was a dynamic site of social media activism, with #Flotilla and #Freedom Flotilla trending after the attack. The social media output of activists was centralized at "Freegaza." Facebook activity was concentrated at "Flotilla For Palestine." This group no longer has a Facebook presence.

55. The IDF video stream was considerable, with over twenty separate videos, most employing English and aimed at an international viewing audience, issued by the army during the first few days following the commando raid. These videos proliferated rapidly in the initial aftermath of the attack on the Flotilla. The cumulative archive includes footage of the original encounter shot from sky and sea, images of the "knives, slingshots, rocks, smoke bombs . . ." found onboard, and images of the "humanitarian cargo" delivered to Gaza by the IDF from the confiscated vessels [see Figure 2.2]. The most viewed among them, that of Navy commandos boarding the Mavi Marmara from helicopter, uploaded on June 2, reached an astonishing 1.2 million views on June 3 alone [see Figure 2.3]. Tsoref, "3 Most Viewed YouTube Clips in the World."

56. The delay was the result of a disagreement between the Israeli foreign ministry and the IDF about the images' potential impact on the nation and on the international public. The IDF feared irrevocable harm to both army morale and the IDF's global reputation. In this window of delay, angry Israeli pundits

noted, the war for hearts and minds was being lost. Horovitz, "Comment: A Scandalous Saga of Withheld Film."

57. Mackey, "Complete Video of Israeli Raid Still Missing."

58. Blumenthal, "IDF Releases Apparently Doctored Flotilla Audio." According to the audio originally released by the IDF, Flotilla activists were alleged to have told the IDF "go back to Auschwitz" and "we're helping Arabs go against the US—don't forget 9/11, guys."

59. "Clarification/Correction Regarding Audio Transmission Between Israeli Navy and Flotilla on 31 May 2010, Posted on 5 June 2010."

60. Kuntsman describes this elsewhere as "anti-humanitarian citizenship," a performance of Israeli citizenship explicitly based on the denial of Palestinian humanitarian need and the framing of any anti-siege or humanitarian action in support of Gaza as an act of terror. "Anti-Humanitarian Citizenship."

61. Issacharoff, Azoulay, Pfeffer, and Khoury, "Protest Flotilla Begins to Move Toward Gaza." Numerous respondents praised the army: "The activists are animals, that's who they are! IDF soldiers, the people are with you—keep up the good work"; "Well done IDF, you are doing God's work—do not let them pass, they just came for nothing, not to help nor to bring food, liars they do not have faith, do not let them pass, good luckkkkkkkkkkkkkk." Shmulik, "IDF: Flotilla Participants Shot and Stabbed with Knives."

62. The clip gave parodic voice to the majority of Israelis who felt misunderstood, abused by a global media that had grossly misconstrued the degree of Gazan suffering and Israeli culpability. Remez, "Caroline Glick's 'We Con the World' and the Tea Partying of the US-Israel Relationship."

63. Tsoref, "Israel Preparing Itself for Twitter War Over Palestinian State."

64. Mizroch, "How Free Explains Israel's Flotilla FAIL."

65. Tsoref, "Israel Preparing Itself for Twitter War Over Palestinian State."

66. For an ethnographic assessment of this shift in state policy toward social media, based on interviews with state officials, see Stein, "StateTube."

67. Grimland, Zrahiya, and Mittelman, "Israel Launches National Cyber Command."

68. State monitoring of Palestinian activists on social media was particularly active in advance of the Nakba day protests of May 2011. The success of such online activism resulted in an Israeli campaign for removal of one offending Facebook group, "The Third Palestinian Intifada" page. Flower, "Facebook Page Supporting Palestinian Intifada Pulled Down."

69. Tsoref, "Israel Preparing Itself for Twitter War Over Palestinian State."

70. For a fuller discussion of the emergence of the vernacular state, see Stein, "StateTube."

71. On so-called "technologies of warning"—more aptly named "technologies of threat"—see "Lawfare in Gaza: Legislative Attack."

72. "From Cast Lead to Pillar of Defense: How the IDF Has Learnt to Communicate War in Gaza Online."

73. "Battleground Twitter (with Images, Tweets)"; Cohen, "In Gaza Conflict, Fighting with Weapons and Postings on Twitter"; Mashable, "The Israel-Gaza Conflict on Twitter."

74. The Facebook initiative sponsored by the Israeli Ministry of Public Diplomacy was the most active patriotic initiative on Facebook at the time, garnering over twenty-five thousand "likes" and over seventy thousand "talking about this" at the time of the military operation. Its core mission was public support for the aerial bombardment and "Israel's right to defend itself," enunciated most famously through cartographic representations of the scale of Hamas fire on southern Israel and in the series of "What would you do?" posters depicting European or American cities under rocket fire and inviting empathy with the war's Israeli victims (its Palestinian victims nowhere in evidence). "The Truth About the Middle East" was a similar Facebook initiative aimed to "conscript [Israelis into] the war efforts." Both of these Facebook projects were widely supported by international Jewish communities. See "Israel Under Fire," and "The Truth About the Middle East." On the state-sponsored Facebook project, see "Bar-Ilan University Students Advocate for Israel During Operation Pillar of Defense."

75. During the course of the incursion, Prime Minister Benjamin Netanyahu used Twitter to thank his country's social media volunteers: "I would like to thank all the citizens of Israel and all over the world who are taking part in the national information effort." Cohen, "In Gaza Conflict, Fighting with Weapons and Postings on Twitter."

76. For examples of personalized images of solidarity posted on Facebook by Israelis, see "ALL the TRUTH about what's happening in ISRAEL's Photos" [sic], accessed November 22, 2012; "Israel Under Fire," Facebook, accessed November 22, 2012; and "The Truth about the Middle East," accessed November 22, 2012. For international examples, see "Israel Under Fire," Facebook, accessed November 21, 2012; "Israel Under Fire," Facebook, accessed November 20, 2012; "Israel en España," Facebook, accessed November 20, 2012.

77. Official state content included playful infographics about Hamas terror and images employing popular social media norms and memes—such as "Keep Calm and Steady On"—even as they conveyed the state's message. Mackey, "Israel's Military Begins Social Media Offensive as Bombs Fall on Gaza."

78. The full poster reads: "Did you know? While Hamas Fires Rockets, Israel Supply Food, Water. Medical Supply and Electricity to Gaza Strip. SHARE THIS

IF YOU AGREE THAT ISRAEL HAS THE RIGHT TO SELF DEFENSE" [sic]. "The Truth About the Middle East."

79. The full text reads: "November 15th, 2012, 8AM—Hamas terrorists in the Gaza Strip launched a salvo of rockets at Israeli population centers throughout southern Israel. They are actively launching the rockets from areas surrounded by Mosques, Kindergartens and public buildings, and using the areas as human shields, knowing that Israel will not return fire on populated civilian areas. November 15th, 2012, 8AM—Israeli air force jets flew over the Gaza Strip, dropped leaflets warning civilians to protect themselves from an impending attack on the area. There is no other army in the world like the Israel Defense Forces (IDF). SHARE THE REALITY OF LIFE IN SOUTHERN ISRAEL, SHARE THE TRUTH" [sic]. "Shay Atik's Photos."

80. The original caption read: "Let's see at least 700 people WHO LOVE THE ISRAELI ARMY" [sic]. It was later changed to: "Like if you love the IDF." Four days into the military operation, this Facebook status had generated over sixty thousand "likes."

81. The Israeli military and pro-Israeli U.S.-based advocacy organizations used the hashtag #IsraelUnderFire heavily during this operation; this hashtag would be used again during Israel's 2014 incursion into the Gaza Strip. On the so-called hashtag wars of 2012, covered extensively in the global media of this period, see Hardy, "#IDF v #Hamas"; "#Israel UnderFire vs. #GazaUnderAttack."

Chapter 3

1. "Capt. Barak Raz Responds to Shameful Facebook Photos Uploaded by Discharged IDF Soldier."

2. Shabi, "Israeli Ex-Soldier Says Facebook Prisoner Pictures Were Souvenirs."

3. Danan, "The Unbearable Lightness of Google+ Enter."

4. The story was first exposed on the Israeli blog *Sachim*. See "Mates, Their Time in the Army Was the Best in Their Lives"; and Reider, "The Best Years of Her Life." The first report of the incident in the Israeli mainstream news was Pereg, "Scandalous Pictures."

5. There was much discussion in the Israeli media of her physicality and sexuality. See the comments on Levanon, "A Soldier 'Modeled' Next to Handcuffed Palestinian Detainees." Many Israeli journalists and bloggers joined the conversation, such as this one who wrote about her "pout" and her carefully plucked eyebrows: Kling, "Days of Our Lives."

6. These translations from the Hebrew appear on Dimi Reider's site. Reider, "Much More Graphic IDF 'Souvenir' Pictures Emerge" and "The Best Years of Her Life."

7. For Israeli media discussion of the event's global coverage, see Dawn, "Soldier from Facebook Captured the World's Headlines." The language of scandal proliferated, as in this headline: "Scandalous Pictures: An IDF Soldier Takes Pictures with Palestinian Detainees." Pereg, "Scandalous Pictures."

8. Danan, "The Unbearable Lightness of Google+ Enter."

9. This phenomenon has been documented by the Israeli NGO Breaking the Silence. See "Soldiers' Photo Exhibit Strikes Nerve." We discuss the organization's involvement in the Abergil affair in what follows. For a general discussion of soldier photography in war contexts, see Struk, *Private Pictures*.

10. Such critiques proliferated in the Israeli media. See, for example, "Minister Edelstein: Goldstone Report Anti-Semitic."

11. Israeli left-wing media pundit Dimi Reider, whose initial post about the Abergil affair set its virality in motion, had this to say about the unfolding viral circuit of the issue: "This has to be the quickest internet shit-storm I ever watched unfold in Israel." Reider, "IDF Officer Poses with Blindfolded Palestinians, Posts Pics on Facebook."

12. Taussig, *Defacement*.

13. Pfeffer, "Web Abuzz Over Soldier's Photos with Bound, Blindfolded Inmates."

14. "Eden Abergil, Poses with Bound Palestinians, Does Not Understand What Is Wrong."

15. In the words of one commenter, "Our enemies don't need to do the damage, we do it ourselves." Danan, "The Unbearable Lightness of Google+ Enter," from the comments section.

16. Mackey, "Israeli Ex-Soldier Defends Her Facebook Snapshots." For a similar critique, see Feiler and Schmulovitch, "Pictures with a Handcuffed Palestinian."

17. On the England-Abergil comparison, see Gurvitz, "Lt. Aberjeel's Sense of Humor." For additional references to Abu Ghraib, see "Eden Abergil and Handcuffed Palestinians—Is Facebook to Blame?" and Yahav, "The Arab Press." On the England comparison, see Dawn, "Soldier from Facebook Captured the World's Headlines." Rarely discussed was Abergil and England's shared social marginality, central to the public disgust they each generated. The racial and class slurs used against Abergil echoed those used against England, herself a working-class white woman who was often described as "white trash" and accused of failing to represent the "real America." For an excellent analysis of England along these lines, see Younge, "Blame the White Trash."

18. In the Israeli media, Arab world coverage was read as an expression of the "sadist culture of the occupation." See Nahmias, "Arab World 'Disgusted' by IDF Facebook Photos." Also see Yahav, "The Arab Press."

19. "Capt. Barak Raz Responds to Shameful Facebook Photos Uploaded by Discharged IDF Soldier." For discussion of this video, see "The Response to the Facebook Photos."

20. Stein, interview with IDF spokesman Captain Barak Raz, Tel Aviv.

21. Such critiques were numerous, although they represented a minority position in Israel. As we note, the Israeli NGO Breaking the Silence was one of the most vocal critics of the affair, encouraging Israelis to understand the episode as part of the everyday condition of occupation. In the words of one of their founders, Yehudah Shaul: "This is commonplace. Don't you take pictures of your everyday life? For these soldiers serving in the occupied territories, this is what they see 24/7—handcuffed and blindfolded Palestinians." Shabi, "Israeli Ex-Soldier Says Facebook Prisoner Pictures Were Souvenirs." A similar critique can be found here: Galon, "Eden Aberjil Also Breaks the Silence." For discussion of the history of such exposures, see Shargal, "We Are All Eden Aberjil."

22. This quote is from Dimi Reider, "Much More Graphic IDF 'Souvenir' Pictures Emerge."

23. Fine, "On Eden Aberjil and the Bite of the Man."

24. Ben-Ami, "Mates, They Don't Mind When Other People Suffer." A similar critique was made by Yonatan Fine, who wrote, "But it is also important to reject apologists on both hands—those who were quick to claim that this is an isolated case . . . A lie; anyone served [in the army] or wandered around the area know that . . . the reality seen from the Facebook page of Abergil is routine." See Fine, "On Eden Aberjil and the Bite of the Man."

25. See Kling, "Days of Our Lives."

26. "Ex-Soldier Presents Cuffed Palestinian Friends."

27. Levanon, "A Soldier 'Modeled' Next to Handcuffed Palestinian Detainees."

28. Israeli military culture and sexism are closely intertwined. Female soldiers in the IDF face structural discrimination, gendered derision, and sexual abuse. And while male soldiers gain symbolic capital as hero-warriors, female soldiers are thus excluded from this economy. Some Israeli commentators argued that Abergil's excessive performance of military violence, both on social media and offline, was the direct result of an army culture that requires female soldiers to act "like the boys" to avoid sexual stigmatization. Kuntsman, personal comments from readers. See also Sasson-Levy, "Gender Performance in a Changing Military."

29. The framing of Abergil as mock cover girl proliferated, as in this headline: "A Soldier Modeled Next to Handcuffed Palestinian Detainees." Levanon, "A Soldier 'Modeled' Next to Handcuffed Palestinian Detainees."

30. The original Facebook post can be found on the group page "We are all with Eden Abergil." The group no longer exists, but snapshots from its homepage can be seen at Harkov, "Facebook Flooded with Photos of Detainees," and Harkov, "'IDF Facebook Photos Are the Norm.'"

31. Kling, "Days of Our Lives."

32. For discussion of performative work of disgust as a way to expel the undesired and maintain the boundaries of a collective, see Ahmed, *The Cultural Politics of Emotion*, and Probyn, *Carnal Appetites*.

33. Left-wing commenters were not exempt from this discourse; indeed, they were among its most vociferous users. For discussion of this aspect, see Fine, "On Eden Aberjil and the Bite of the Man."

34. Notable exceptions to this race-blind discourse included "Eden Abergil, Racism and Patriarchy"; Fine, "On Eden Aberjil and the Bite of the Man"; and Gabbay, "Whose Blindfold Is This?" Also see comments to "I Understood What's Wrong, I Apologized to Those Who Were Hurt."

35. "Eden Aberjil and Handcuffed Palestinians—Is Facebook to Blame?"

36. Pereg, "Scandalous Pictures"; see also Danan, "The Unbearable Lightness of Google+ Enter."

37. Here are the words of one Israeli commenter: "I am amazed by the power of the Net and how exposed we all are; every piece of information from our past can come back to us at any time, threatening us and leaving us completely exposed before the onlooker. I am also amazed by one's ability to respond, to judge and to threaten the life of someone via the net, even with a light hand on the keyboard." Danan, "The Unbearable Lightness of Google+ Enter."

38. As one blogger wrote, "The Edens of this world fail to distinguish between the public and the private. They don't know that walls became transparent. Five years ago, no one was exposed to the disgusting experiences of Eden from the army service, except for one's parents and friends." Shargal, "We Are All Eden Aberjil."

39. Pereg, "Scandalous Pictures"; see also Danan, "The Unbearable Lightness of Google+ Enter."

40. Sadan, "IDF's Facebook Dilemma." Others proposed that "[m]any IDF soldiers forget the viral power of the net." Grimland, "Israeli' PR's Hottest Merchandise—Eden Abergil."

41. Danan, "The Unbearable Lightness of Google+ Enter," in the comments section.

42. Ibid. Others drew attention to the security risks associated with Abergil's images, noting that "[a]lso visible in the former soldier's photographs were the field headquarters where she was stationed, with military maps and documents

on the walls, including what appears to be classified material." Pfeffer, "Web Abuzz Over Soldier's Photos with Bound, Blindfolded Inmates." Others noted that such exposures made classified IDF information accessible to state enemies. See the comments on "I Understood What's Wrong, I Apologized to Those Who Were Hurt."

43. "IDF Soldier Posts Images of Blindfolded Palestinians on Facebook, from 'Best Time of My Life.'"

44. Ibid.

45. In this rendering, "humiliation" pivots on the lack of permission granted while the legalistic language of "right to privacy" is foregrounded as a way to restore the humanity to the Palestinian subjects in question. The restoration of *this* right is imagined as a foremost means of restoring justice—rather than, say, via the human rights of the Palestinian subject in question.

46. The director of the Public Committee Against Torture employed a "right to privacy" language to argue his position: "The horrible pictures demonstrate a norm of treating Palestinians like objects instead of human beings—treatment that disregards their feelings as humans and *their right to privacy. . . .* The soldier would go crazy if photographs of her in humiliating circumstances had been posted on the internet without her permission. We call upon IDF commanders to issue orders to prevent this kind of humiliating behavior." "IDF Soldier Posts Images of Blindfolded Palestinians on Facebook, from 'Best Time of My Life.'"

47. Feiler and Schmulovitch, "Pictures with a Handcuffed Palestinian"; "My Life Was Threatened Because of the Photos."

48. For a review of these memes, see Ben Israel, "Eden Abergil—The Web-surfers Version." For general discussion of meme logics and norms, see Shifman, "An Anatomy of a YouTube Meme."

49. Breaking the Silence is an organization of veteran Israeli combat soldiers who run a testimonial project about army violence in Palestinian territories.

50. Ha'aretz described the images this way: "several graphic photos depicting soldiers posing next to the bodies of suspected militants as well as next to hand-cuffed detainees [viewer discretion is advised]." "'Facebook Photos of Soldiers Posing with Bound Palestinians Are the Norm.'"

51. In keeping with privacy protocols, the organization chose to pixilate the faces of the soldiers, leaving only their smiles intact. The international media would often pixilate the faces of the Palestinians.

52. Breaking the Silence noted the following on their Facebook page: "Un-surprisingly, the IDF spokesman released a 'shocked' statement saying that this is the 'shameless and ugly behavior of one soldier.' This picture is not the ugly behavior of one person, but a norm throughout the army." Harkov, "'IDF

Facebook Photos Are the Norm.'" The intervention of Breaking the Silence would catalyze the exposure of other violent military images on social media, some of which went viral. Many of these perpetrator-circulated images had celebratory captions, such as the following (below an image of Border Police repression): "This is the only language the Arabs understand, your next Nakba is comming soon. Inshallah." See Breiner, "Humiliating Palestinians on FaceBook."

53. Many Israeli social media users objected to this comparison, as they noted in numerous Facebook posts, "Look what the Americans do in the Iraqi prison, how can you compare this to Abergil, she has not humiliated anyone, only took a picture!" "Fan Photos from We Are All with Eden Abergil."

54. This Facebook group originally identified itself as a right-wing solidarity initiative with Abergil. But its political aims were soon questioned when links to anti-occupation activism on its Facebook feed raised suspicion. Soon, a rival Facebook page was created to denounce the initiative as anti-Israeli. "Israelis Do Not Join the Radical Leftist Group 'We Are All with Eden Abergil.'" The group no longer exists, but snapshots from its homepage can be seen at Harkov, "Facebook Flooded with Photos of Detainees."

55. Harkov, "Facebook Flooded with Photos of Detainees."

56. Twibbon is a web-based application that overlays an image of choice onto one's Twitter or Facebook profile. See "About Us."

57. Emphasis ours. The Twibbon image in question was available at "Eden Abergil—Support Campaign."

58. Reider, "Eden Abergil Gets Meme Treatment." This body of memes would generate extensive commentary within national and international media outlets. "Eden Abergil, Meet the Nation Website."

59. In other memes, the blindfolded detainees were replaced by Israeli political figures (Bibi Netanyahu, Ehud Barak, and Avegdor Liberman).

60. Abramov and Agabareeya, "We Are Eden's Backdrop," and Yossi Gurvitz, "Lt. Aberjeel's Sense of Humor."

61. This legal decision was also extended to other cases of soldiers who photographed themselves with Palestinian detainees and uploaded their trophies to social networks. See Glickman, "'Facebook Soldier' Won't Be Probed," and "State Won't Prosecute Eden Abergil for Facebook Photos."

62. Perhaps the most viral such incident involved Itai Wallach, an Israeli contestant in a popular Israeli reality TV series, whose Facebook page includes images of Wallach with arms around blindfolded Palestinian detainees. After the images were discovered in 2013, Wallach issued a tearful apology to the public and his mother, describing the photos as an innocent, youthful mistake.

He also assured Israelis that the two blindfolded men were "wanted terrorists," noting that he had, nonetheless, "treated them well." "I Am Ashamed of the Picture and Regret It."

63. "Video of Naked Soldiers Goes Viral."

64. For a recent articulation of army policy as it pertains to Facebook, see Cohen, "A New Directive Will Impose Restrictions IDF Soldiers' Use of Facebook."

65. The Abergil precedent was frequently invoked during the viral Wallach affair (see note 62). "During his military service, he found the time to do what the soldier Eden Abergil did." "Scandal: 'Big Brother' Contestant Photographed with Bound Palestinians."

66. "Eden Abergil and Handcuffed Palestinians—Is Facebook to Blame?"

67. Danan, "The Unbearable Lightness of Google+ Enter," in the comments section.

Chapter 4

1. "A Dead Man Came to Life in Gaza."

2. Harkov, "Hamas Co-Opts Photos of Injured Syrians," emphasis ours.

3. Yaron, "Tip: How to Recognize a Fake Photograph."

4. Ibid.

5. Harkov, "Hamas Co-Opts Photos of Injured Syrians."

6. The following anonymous web commentator, writing for Zionism-Israel .com, articulates the sentiment succinctly: "[Numerous scholars have] insisted that the exodus of Palestinian refugees was due only to Zionist violence, and insinuated or stated that the violence was part of a planned policy to evict the Arabs of Palestine. A large number of quotes and documents have been doctored or fabricated and advanced by either side as 'evidence.' Some of these can be verified. Others appear with different dates in different places and are suspicious. None of them provide conclusive proof." Isseroff, "The Palestine Nakba Controversy."

7. For more discussion of the incredulity of the Palestinian eyewitness, see Stein, "Impossible Witness."

8. See, for example, Benjamin, *The Work of Art in the Age of Mechanical Reproduction*; Mitchell, *The Reconfigured Eye*; and Morris, *Believing Is Seeing*.

9. Concerns about authenticity and the "real" have been an integral part of cyberculture over the past several decades, immortalized in the much-cited *New Yorker* cartoon, "On the Internet, nobody knows you're a dog." Steiner, "On the Internet, Nobody Knows You're a Dog." For more discussion of this issue, see the voluminous debate that followed the death of Neda Sultan in Iran,

2006, and the "A Gay Girl in Damascus" cyberhoax. We discuss the latter in more detail in Kuntsman and Stein, "Digital Suspicion, Politics, and the Middle East." Also see "Famous Internet Hoaxes"; Malkowski, "Streaming Death"; and Zuckerman, "Understanding #amina." For additional academic discussions of these issues, see Kuntsman, "Written in Blood," and Stone, "Will the Real Body Please Stand up?"

10. For an example of digital suspicion by means of digital verification tools, consider the example of "Checkdesk," "an open source fact-checking workbench for global new media." "Checkdesk: A New Approach to Fact-Checking Citizen Media of the Arab Spring."

11. Digital suspicion was enabled by the proliferation of Internet-based search tools such as Google Images or TinEar.

12. For a full discussion of the scale of the death and damage wrought by Pillar of Defense, see Stein, *Human Rights Violations During Operation Pillar of Defense, 14–21 November 2012.*

13. On Israeli militarization after 2000, see Beinin and Stein, *The Struggle for Sovereignty*, 48.

14. Israel's official press release on the al-Dura affair can be seen at "Publication of the Government Review Committee Report Regarding Al-Durrah on France Channel 2." Much has been written on the government's endorsement of the hoax hypothesis. See, for example, Derfner, "On the Al-Dura Affair." For general discussion of the case within the Israeli media, see Magnezi, "Was Al-Dura Video Fabricated?" and Somfalvi, "Israeli Committee: Al-Dura Alive at End of Video."

15. *Jenin: IDF Military Operations*; *Shielded from Scrutiny: IDF Violations in Jenin and Nablus.*

16. There was no single emblematic image of this military operation.

17. The film was produced by Palestinian Israeli actor and filmmaker Mohammad Bakri. Bakri would be sued for defamation, and the film vilified as a hoax and banned by the Israeli Film Board. The ban was overturned by the Israeli Supreme Court, which argued that "[t]he fact that the film includes lies is not enough to justify a ban." "Israel's Court Defeats Film Ban."

18. On the first Photoshop war, see Mor, "The First Photoshop War." Scholarship on the Lebanese case includes Cooper, "A Concise History of the Fauxtography Blogstorm in the 2006 Lebanon War," and Usher, "Reviewing Fauxtography." For an extended meditation on the question and history of photographic evidence, including discussion of the Lebanese case, see Morris, *Believing Is Seeing.*

19. The Lebanese case is also marshaled as a cautionary tale about do-it-yourself digital forensics. See Daniel, *Digital Forensics for Legal Professionals.*

20. Lappin, "Reuters Admits to More Image Manipulation." U.S.-based blogger Charles Johnson of littlegreenfootballs.com exposed Reuters' hoax. He explained, "This is almost certainly caused by using the Photoshop 'clone' tool to add more smoke to the image." See Johnson, "Reuters Doctoring Photos from Beirut?"

21. Lappin, "New York Times 'Used Fraudulent Photo.'"

22. Ibid.

23. The exposure of so-called hoaxes associated with the Qana air strikes can be found at Landes, "The Corruption of the Media." After charging Reuters with publicizing a fraudulent charge about the image of a dead Lebanese man in Qana, some U.S.-based bloggers and journalists were forced to issue an apology, noting that he was actually dead. Landes, "Post on Washington Post Removed."

24. Lappin, "New York Times 'Used Fraudulent Photo.'" Several right-wing U.S.-based pro-Israel lobbies were involved in disseminating the suspicion charge during the Lebanon 2006 war—chief among them "Camera" [The Committee for Accuracy in Middle East Reporting in America]; "Honest Reporting"; and "Israel Project." See Hollander, "Iran Does It Again: Faked Missile Reminiscent of 'Green Helmet Guy' and Other Staged News Events"; "The Media's Coverage of the Conflict in the North"; and "Updated: A Reprise: Media Photo Manipulation."

25. Mor, "The First Photoshop War." On the use of digital manipulation to harm the national image, see Lappin, "AP Beirut Photo Faces Questions." The Israeli press charged the global media, particularly the British press, with an "anti-Israel tirade" where Lebanon was concerned, of which doctoring charges were deemed an integral part. Lappin, "Israeli War Deaths Go Largely Unnoticed."

26. As we noted in Chapter 2, the Israeli incursion took place in the context of an Israeli state-imposed ban on the entry of foreign journalists into Gaza, although many reported from within Israel, near the Gaza border. The burden of testimonial was therefore transferred to Palestinian residents and the few internationals working in Gaza, mainly doctors and humanitarian agents—that is, to the relatively small numbers with Internet access and social media literacy, the former crippled by frequent electricity outrage. At the time of the incursion, most Jewish Israelis were reliant on national newspapers and television, filled with stories and images of Israeli suffering and little reporting on Gazan fatalities and devastation. Those active on international news resources on the Internet were facing—and responding to—a very different visual and affective field; many took it as their patriotic mission to challenge the narrative of Palestinian victimhood by disregarding the photographs as staged or Photoshopped. Many Russian Israelis, for example, were active in the transnational Russian-language blogosphere, where they deployed the same charges of staging and digital fakery

that we would later see en masse about Hebrew-speaking Israelis in 2012. On the terms of this constrained Israeli media field, and the anomalous figure of the Palestinian witness, see Stein, "Impossible Witness." On the rejection of Palestinian victimhood by diasporic Russian-Israelis during the 2008–2009 Israeli incursion, see Kuntsman, "Digital Archives of Feelings and Their Haunted Futures."

27. The claim that Palestinians stage their injuries for the camera—a charge noted in shorthand as the "Pallywood" phenomenon, meaning a Hollywood style propaganda—is attributable to Boston University professor Richard Landes, who has, since the time of the al-Dura killing, engaged in an active media campaign to expose instances of Palestinian fraudulence to the global media. He defines the Pallywood phenomenon this way: "The Palestinians regularly fabricate scenes for TV cameras, which, when sent to Western media outlets, are cut down to the believable three-second sight bite. And what makes it to the evening news is a stringing together of these staged scenes." Morris, "Ruthie Blum Interviews Richard Landes." Landes tracks the history of the phenomenon to the 1982 Lebanon war; see "The Second Draft." The success of Landes' media campaign resulted in the Israeli government's 2013 endorsement of the fraudulence charge where the al-Dura killing was concerned.

28. See Ahikam, "Due to the Reviews in the World," and Landau, "Israel Gives Up White Phosphorus, Because 'It Doesn't Photograph Well.'"

29. The case in question involved the Samur family of Jabalya. According to Human Rights Watch, the truck targeted by the Israeli military drone was carrying oxygen canisters for welding purposes. In their discussion of the case, Human Rights Watch pointed out the inaccuracies and mismatches between the videos released by the IDF and their official declarations, all on the basis of a detailed analysis of the video. HRW argued that the drone's visual equipment should have been able to present a clear picture and that the video contradicts the IDF story. See *Precisely Wrong: Gaza Civilians Killed by Israeli Drone-Launched Missles.* The video can be screened at "Underground Weapons Storage Facility in Gaza Struck by Israel Air Force."

30. State representatives from the Israeli Foreign Ministry countered that Israeli military cameras had merely been inaccurately set. Stein interview, Israeli Foreign Ministry, Jerusalem.

31. These charges took particular aim at the IDF's Twitter and Facebook accounts, where such claims were frequently made. See Eglash, "#IsraelUnderFire from Gaza Plays Out on Twitter." Also see the IDF's official blog during Pillar of Defense, under the heading "Israel Under Fire."

32. One example is a Facebook poster comparing two identical photographs of a bombing site in Gaza, the first taken in January 2009 and the second in

November 2012. The poster appeared on Facebook on November 15, 2012, and was reposted over seven thousand times and liked by over fifteen hundred people. "Compare and contrast," says the poster, listing the dates and details of the two images, and warning readers to "beware of propaganda." Many similar posters and comparisons appeared on the Facebook walls of "Israel Under Fire" and "Truth About the Middle East."

33. The Facebook page of StandWithUs UK exposed "[t]he BBC's Jon Donnison [who was] caught posting photos of Syria and passing them off as from Gaza." See "StandWIthUs UK's Photos."

34. Leibowitz, "Lies, Folks."

35. Ben-Israel, "Caught Red-Handed."

36. "A Good Picture Is Worth a Thousand Words?" On the dangers of Facebook "likes," see Elbaz, "The War for 'Likes.'"

37. Harkov, "Hamas Co-Opts Photos of Injured Syrians."

38. This was merely one instance of a widespread campaign by Israeli bloggers, Internet surfers, and members of the Israeli military's own new-media team who searched for bloody images that had been recirculated on social media out of context. The original Facebook exposure can be found at "Shay Atik's Photos." See also Maputo, "After the Attack," and "Operation Pillar of Defense: Hamas Distorts Photos and Videos, the BBC Is Misled, and the Picture Translated by Shai Atik Goes Viral on Facebook." Also see Ben-Israel, "Caught Red-Handed."

39. Pro-Israeli media sleuths, largely U.S.-based, had detected the man walking unassisted in subsequent footage—"a dead man came to life," in the sarcastic words of one suspicious Israeli blogger. "A Dead Man Came to Life in Gaza." See also "Miraculous Recovery by Injured Gaza Man?" But many disagreed with this proposition. A blogger who meticulously analyzed the footage wrote, "What exactly do we have? Well, nothing really—no smoking gun, no definitive proof of staging or fakery, nor is there proof that there wasn't staging or fakery. I can say this with confidence after spending hours reviewing each & every frame." "About That So-Called 'Pallywood' Video . . ."

40. Nelson, "World Press Photo of the Year 2013."

41. Harkov, "Hamas Co-Opts Photos of Injured Syrians." In one case, suspicious Israeli readers charged Palestinian bloggers with repurposing an image of a Palestinian child injured by Hamas rocket fire, reframed as an Israeli-inflicted injury. Ibid.

42. The fraudulence charge was originally exposed on Extremetech.com, a website working with image forensics. Unlike most Israeli suspicious readings, this one employed a highly technical toolbox. As per the article, "There were two main stages to the analysis: First an interrogation of the JPEG's XMP block,

which details the file's Photoshop save history, and then pixel-level error level analysis (ELA). . . ." Anthony, "Was the 2013 World Press Photo of the Year Faked with Photoshop, or Merely Manipulated?"

43. The photograph was examined by the digital photography experts of World Press and its integrity confirmed. They wrote, "We have reviewed the RAW image, as supplied by World Press Photo, and the resulting published JPEG image. It is clear that the published photo was retouched with respect to both global and local color and tone. Beyond this, however, we find no evidence of significant photo manipulation or compositing. Furthermore, the analysis purporting photo manipulation is deeply flawed, as described briefly below." The full report can be found at "Digital Photography Experts Confirm the Integrity of Paul Hansen's Image Files."

44. See the online comments responding to "Was the 'Picture of the Year' of a Children's Funeral in Gaza Fabricated?"

45. Ibid.

46. Harkov, "Hamas Co-Opts Photos of Injured Syrians."

47. In the process, cyberspace was being nationalized. For work on the nationalization of cyberspace, see Everard, *Virtual States*; Khalili, "Virtual Nation"; Kuntsman, *Figurations of Violence and Belonging*; and Mitra, "Virtual Commonality."

48. On Israeli national media coverage of the 2008–2009 incursion, including the systematic refusal to engage with the figure of the Palestinian victim, see Stein, "Impossible Witness," and Orgad, "Watching How Others Watch Us."

49. "Was the 'Picture of the Year' of a Children's Funeral in Gaza Fabricated?" See the comments section.

50. One social media expert put it this way: "Using online research tools to dig into history and reveal the truth is very effective." Harkov, "Hamas Co-Opts Photos of Injured Syrians."

Chapter 5

1. Yaron, "IDF Soldier Posts Instagram Photo of Palestinian Boy in Crosshairs of Sniper Rifle."

2. Blau, "Israeli Troops Humiliate Palestinians—and Put It on YouTube."

3. Manekin, "What Youtube Finds Offensive."

4. Many Hebrew-language commentators on social media lauded the abuse.

5. Through the memoirs of former Israeli border policemen, this performance can be traced to at least the early 1990s, when it functioned as a comic companion to the repressive violence of the Israeli security services during the first Palestinian uprising. Today, forcing Palestinians to perform retains its popu-

larity within the Israeli armed service, employed when soldiers are bored and particularly when Palestinians are detained, and often filmed for personal and platoon enjoyment ("so they can boast to the guys and show it to friends in civilian life"). Breaking the Silence, cited in Blau, "Israeli Troops Humiliate Palestinians—and Put It on YouTube." For a discussion of prior instances of this practice, see Halevi, *At the Entrance to the Garden of Eden.*

6. This incident is part of a transnational practice, called (in the U.K. context) "happy slapping": filming and publishing videos or images of violent attacks. See Saunders, "Happy Slapping," and Yar, "Crime, Media and the Will-to-Representation."

7. Blau, "Israeli Troops Humiliate Palestinians—and Put It on YouTube."

8. Ali Abunimah runs and writes for the Electronic Intifada website. See Abunimah, "Israeli Soldier Posts Disturbing Instagram Photo of Child in Crosshairs of His Rifle."

9. This image resonates with Sontag's famous observations about the ways that cameras function as weapons. In this Instagram instance, the sniper's rifle and the smartphone were brought into an intimate collaboration. Sontag, *On Photography.* Other classic texts on the ways cameras function as wartime tools include Morris, *Believing Is Seeing*; and Virilio, *War and Cinema.* See also Alper, "War on Instagram."

10. Abunimah, "Israeli Soldier Posts Disturbing Instagram Photo of Child in Crosshairs of His Rifle."

11. Doherty, "War Sporno"; Zitun, "Soldiers Disciplined for Mistreating Palestinian Detainees."

12. Other military spokesmen took recourse to the discourse of "digital suspicion" (Chapter 4) to undercut the incident's import: "According to IDF sources, it was not proven that the soldier actually took the photograph himself, saying that it is possible he found it online and decided to upload it to his account. The photograph could even be fake, they said." Zitun, "Soldiers Disciplined for Mistreating Palestinian Detainees."

13. For a discussion of Israeli warfare and the gendering of Palestinian victims, see Mikdashi, "Can Palestinian Men Be Victims?"

14. Yaron, "IDF Soldier Posts Instagram Photo of Palestinian Boy in Crosshairs of Sniper Rifle."

15. "Soldiers' Dance in Hebron May Mean Trouble." This video, originally titled "Batallion 50 Rock the Hebron Casbah" or "Tic Tock," featured Israeli soldiers from Nahal Brigade's 50th Airborne Battalion, dancing in occupied Hebron. It was removed from YouTube by its creator after its initial exposure but would be promptly reposted under different names. This event, one of the first viral

scandals of its time involving military usage of social media, produced prolific commentary in the Israeli media, including an expose from the vantage of the Palestinian residents of Hebron who had watched the performance in real time. "Rock the Casba—IDF Soldiers Dancing in Hebron." We discuss the reception of this video in greater detail at Kuntsman and Stein, "Digital Suspicion, Politics, and the Middle East."

16. "Female IDF Soldiers Punished for Racy Photos." The following viral scandal featuring female soldiers would break one week later. "Video of Naked Soldiers Goes Viral."

17. Abunimah, "Israeli Soldier Posts Disturbing Instagram Photo of Child in Crosshairs of His Rifle"; Abunimah, "Stoned, Naked, Armed and Dangerous."

18. Schechter, "The Social Intifada." Soldiers regularly retool their smart-phones as surveillance tools in the field of military operations. See Zonszein, "WATCH: IDF Does Not Want You to See What Occupation Looks Like."

19. "IDF Plans Social Media Clampdown for Soldiers."

20. Recent academic analyses of the selfie genre include Fausing, "Selfies and the Search for Recognition"; Piela, "I Am Just Doing My Bit to Promote Modesty"; Rettberg, "Freshly Generated for You, and Barack Obama"; Senft, "Epistemology of the Second Selfie"; and Vivienne and Burgess, "The Remediation of the Personal Photograph and the Politics of Self-Representation in Digital Storytelling."

21. The Israeli NGO Breaking the Silence has provided the fullest documentation of this militarized genre in the Israeli context. For a broader discussion of military souvenir portraiture, see Arbuthnot, "Military Deviancy, War 'Trophies'"; and Struk, *Private Pictures*.

22. Following this exposure, social media sleuths found tens of similar images on Instagram, also photographed and uploaded by Israeli soldiers and also employing standard Instagram protocols to aestheticize military practices.

23. Cohen, "Israeli Soldier Aims Gun at Teen in Video Clip." The Palestinian activist involved in the original incident and responsible for the footage, Issa Amro, was harassed by the Israeli military for months after the event. See Zonszein, "PHOTO: Soldier Punches Palestinian Activist in the Face."

24. Harel and Cohen, "The IDF's First Digital Rebellion."

25. "Even on Independence Day: Protest Against the Restraint Policy Continues."

26. "Israeli Justice."

27. Golan, "Senior Figure in the IDF on the Protests Which Began on 0404."

28. Golan, "IDF Soldiers Started a Protest Against A Suspended Soldier Who Pointed a Weapon at an Arab in Hebron"; Margalit and Zitun, "Suspended Nahal Soldier Finds Online Support for His Reinstatement"; "Talk of the Day:

'David Nahlawi' as a National Hero"; Weiss and Lango, "An Officer in the Army Spokesman's Unit Admits: The Soldiers' Protest Is Justified."

29. Ben-Yishai, "IDF Must Put an End to Virtual Protest." Some Israeli media pundits understood the internal protest differently, speaking of the ways it might enable a culture of accountability within the military: "[To] the young soldiers who carry smartphones alongside their army-issued rifles, the phone is more than a fun apparatus. Their phones are their personal weapons against wrongdoing, including by the army." Schechter, "The Social Intifada."

30. The army elected not to take punitive actions against the soldiers who joined the mass social media protest, despite their violation of IDF social media protocols.

31. "Former-IDF Censor: I Also Have Revealing Photos."

32. On the history of the investment in the power of both social media and the camera to effect social change, see Gregory, "Cameras Everywhere." For a discussion of how the Western activist investment in the smartphone as witness has played out in the context of the Syrian civil war—said to be the most socially mediated war in history—see Lynch, Freelon, and Aday, *Syria's Socially Mediated Civil War.*

33. Anonymization was a somewhat fictional protection, as many of these images had been tagged on Facebook.

Afterword

1. Schechter, "Selfies in the Service of Hate.

2. Ibid.

3. One U.S. pundit wrote, during the course of the incursion, "Social media have helped allow us to see more deeply inside war zones—in this case, inside Gaza—and allowed viewers much fuller access to the terror that grips a population under military attack." Wallace-Wells, "Why Israel Is Losing the American Media War." This sentiment was shared by many, including reporter David Carr. Carr, "At Front Lines, Bearing Witness in Real Time."

4. For discussion along these lines, see "Social Media: The Weapon of Choice in the Gaza-Israel Conflict."

5. "Hotline, That's What I Have?"

6. Bi'our and Weisburg, "'Death to Arabs'"; Cook, "Israel's Gaza Backlash Targets Arab Minority"; "Protective Edge: The War of Reports on Facebook"; Tsuk, "Online Incitement."

7. Baharir, "Israelis Launch Facebook Campaign Calling for 'Revenge' of Teens' Murders"; Schechter, "Selfies in the Service of Hate."

8. Hasson, "Murder of Palestinian Teen Was No 'Honor Killing,' Says His Family."

9. Kershner, "6 Israelis Held Over the Killing of Palestinian."

10. In a variant of digital suspicion, Prime Minister Netanyahu infamously accused Hamas of using images of the Palestinian dead as a public relations tool. In his words, "They want to pile up as many civilian dead as they can. . . . They use telegenically dead Palestinians for their cause. They want the more dead, the better." See Weiner, "Netanyahu: Hamas Wants 'Telegenically Dead Palestinians.'"

11. This analysis of the complex temporality of a photograph draws on Roland Barthes' meditation on the "anterior future" of the photograph of impending death. See Barthes, *Camera Lucida*. For a critical reading of Barthes on this point, see Butler, *Frames of War*.

12. Fabian, *Time and the Other*.

13. In the Israeli case, secrecy is also preserved through another temporal idiom: the temporary. See Ariella Azoulay and Adi Ophir on the fictive temporariness of the military occupation, and how this prevailing fiction functions to maintain the occupation as status quo. Azoulay and Ophir, *The One-State Condition*, 15.

14. On security discourses and practices in everyday Israel, see Ochs, *Security and Suspicion: An Ethnography of Everyday Life in Israel*.

15. Livni, "Israel's Lot after the Gaza War."

16. Weitz, "Signs of Fascism in Israel Reached New Peak During Gaza Op, Says Renowned Scholar."

17. Awad, "Where Do We Go from Here?" Discussions about the unraveling of liberal Zionism were particularly active within the American Jewish community. See Schechter, "Liberal Zionism." For many Israeli commentators on both the Israeli left and right, the receding Israeli future was also tied to the unraveling two-state solution. Ahren, "The Rocket That Spelled the End of the Two-State Solution?"

18. Our work draws on a large body of scholarship on the interplay between archives, memory, and digitality—much of which correlates with the work of Derrida, *Archive Fever*. See, for example, Eichorn, "Archival Genres: Gathering Texts and Reading Spaces"; Garde-Hansen, Hoskins, and Reading, *Save As . . . Digital Memories*; "Issue 4. War, Conflict and Commemoration in the Age of Digital Reproduction"; Mayer-Schönberger, *Delete: The Virtue of Forgetting in the Digital Age*; and Wolfgang, *Digital Memory and the Archive*. On digital archives, haunted futurities, and political justice, see also Kuntsman, "Digital Archives of Feelings and Their Haunted Futures."

19. As this book was moving into production, there were increasing conversations among new media analysts about the mutability of digital archives,
including the efforts of U.S. social networking sites and private web specialists
to remove offending and incriminating social media content. In response, some
human rights organizations proposed that perpetrator footage be preserved in
a "digital 'evidence locker' [that] would make sure that powerful but offensive
citizen media related to human rights is downloaded and saved. This would be
done in a way that preserves metadata and other important video information,
so that it can potentially be used in future prosecutions and investigations by
NGOs and human rights actors." On efforts to remove offending content, see
Chen, "The Laborers Who Keep Dick Pics and Beheadings Out of Your Facebook Feed." On online image fixers and the mutability of digital archives, see
Toobin, "The Solace of Oblivion." On the digital "evidence locker," see Gregory,
"Images of Horror: Whose Roles and What Responsibility?"

Bibliography

@AlqassamBrigade. Twitter post, November 14, 2012, 11:04 A.M. https://twitter
    .com/AlqassamBrigade/status/268791630583193600.

@IDFSpokesman. Twitter post, November 14, 2012, 6:29 A.M. https://twitter
    .com/IDFSpokesperson/status/268722403989925888.

@Joseph_in_OC. Twitter post, November 14, 2012, 9:03 P.M. https://twitter
    .com/Joseph_in_OC/status/268942246877990912.

"#IsraelUnderFire vs. #GazaUnderAttack." *Storify*. Accessed July 30, 2014. http://
    storify.com/globalpost/israelunderfire-vs-gazaunderattack.

Abdel-Latif, Omayma. "It's War—Virtually." *Al-Ahram*, November 2, 2000. http://
    weekly.ahram.org.eg/2000/506/re7.htm.

"About That So-Called 'Pallywood' Video." *Little Green Footballs*, November
    17, 2012. http://littlegreenfootballs.com/article/41210_About_That_So-
    Called_Pallywood_Video.

"About Us." *Twibbon*. Accessed August 17, 2013. http://twibbon.com/about.

Abramov, Eti, and Iman Agabareeya. "We Are Eden's Backdrop." *Yediot Aharonot*, September 2, 2010. http://www.scribd.com/doc/36790248/Eden-Avergil
    24hours.

Abunimah, Ali. "Stoned, Naked, Armed and Dangerous: More Disturbing Images from an Israeli Soldier's Instagram." *The Electronic Intifada*, February 20,
    2013. http://electronicintifada.net/blogs/ali-abunimah/stoned-naked-armed-and
    -dangerous-more-disturbing-images-israeli-soldiers.

———. "Israeli Soldier Posts Disturbing Instagram Photo of Child in Crosshairs of His Rifle." *The Electronic Intifada*, February 15, 2013. http://elect
    ronicintifada.net/blogs/ali-abunimah/israeli-soldier-posts-disturbing-insta
    gram-photo-child-crosshairs-his-rifle.

AbuZayyad, Ziad Khalil. "Human Rights, the Internet and Social Media: Has
Technology Changed the Way We See Things?" *Palestine—Israel Journal of
Politics, Economics, and Culture* 18, no. 4 (2013): 38–40.

Acar, Adam. "Culture, Corruption, Suicide, Happiness and Global Social Media Use: A Cross-Cultural Perspective." *International Journal of Web-Based Communities* 10, no. 3 (2014): 357–400.

Ahikam, David Moshe. "Due to the Reviews in the World: A Separate IDF Phosphorus." *NRG*, April 25, 2013. http://www.nrg.co.il/online/1/ART2/463/591.html.

Ahmed, Sara. *The Cultural Politics of Emotion*. Edinburgh: Edinburgh University Press, 2004.

Ahren, Raphael. "The Rocket That Spelled the End of the Two-State Solution?" *Times of Israel*, August 10, 2014. http://www.timesofisrael.com/the-rocket-that-spelled-the-end-of-the-two-state-solution.

Aikins, Stephen Kwamena, and Christopher G. Reddick. *Web 2.0 Technologies and Democratic Governance: Political, Policy and Management Implications*. New York: Springer, 2012.

Akrivopoulou, Christina, and Nicolaos Garipidis. *Digital Democracy and the Impact of Technology on Governance and Politics: New Globalized Practices*. Igi Global, 2013.

"ALL the TRUTH about what happening in ISRAEL's Photos." Facebook. Accessed November 22, 2012, https://www.facebook.com/photo.php?fbid=524258444253577&set=a.220210174658407.63897.202904329722325&type=1&relevant_count=1.

Allan, Diana, and Curtis Brown. "The Mavi Marmara at the Frontlines of Web 2.0." *Journal of Palestine Studies* 40, no. 1 (Autumn 2010): 63–77.

Allen, Patrick D., and Chris C. Demchak. "The Palestinian-Israeli Cyberwar." *Military Review* 83, no. 2 (March 1, 2003): 52.

Alper, Meryl. "War on Instagram: Framing Conflict Photojournalism with Mobile Photography Apps." *New Media & Society*, September 18, 2013.

Al-Rizzo, Hasan M. "The Undeclared Cyberspace War Between Hezbollah and Israel." *Contemporary Arab Affairs* 1 (2008): 391–405.

Alsaafin, Linah. "Palestinians Turn to Facebook in Fight Against Occupation." *Al-Monitor*, April 25, 2013. http://www.al-monitor.com/pulse/originals/2013/04/social-media-palestinian-activism.html.

Anduiza, Eva, Michael James Jensen, and Laia Jorba. *Digital Media and Political Engagement Worldwide: A Comparative Study*. Cambridge: Cambridge University Press, 2012.

Anthony, Sebastian. "Was the 2013 World Press Photo of the Year Faked with Photoshop, or Merely Manipulated?" *Extremetech*, May 13, 2013. http://www.extremetech.com/extreme/155617-how-the-2013-world-press-photo-of-the-year-was-faked-with-photoshop.

Aouragh, Miriyam. "Framing the Internet in the Arab Revolutions: Myth Meets Modernity." *Cinema Journal* 52, no. 1 (2012): 148–56.

———. "Confined Offline, Traversing Online Palestinian Mobility Through the Prism of the Internet." *Mobilities* 6, no. 3 (September 2011): 375–97.

———. *Palestine Online?: Transnationalism, the Internet and the Construction of Identity*. London; New York: I.B. Tauris Academic Studies, 2011.

———. "Virtual Intifada: Online Activism and Everyday Resistance." *Journal of Arab and Muslim Media Research* 1, no. 2 (2008): 109–30.

Arbuthnot, Felicity. "Military Deviancy, War 'Trophies': Body Parts and Souvenir Stars and Stripes from Predator Drones." *Global Research*, July 26, 2013. http://www.globalresearch.ca/military-deviancy-and-war-trophies-body-parts-fore arms-and-souvenir-stars-and-stripes-from-predator-drones/5343963.

Archibald, David, and Mitchell Miller. "Full-Spectacle Dominance? An Analysis of the Israeli State's Attempts to Control Media Images of the 2010 Gaza Flotilla." *Journal of War & Culture Studies* 5, no. 2 (October 25, 2012): 189–201. doi:10.1386/jwcs.5.2.189_1.

Ashuri, Tamar. "(Web)sites of Memory and the Rise of Moral Mnemonic Agents." *New Media & Society* 14, no. 3 (May 1, 2012): 441–56.

Asthana, Sanjay, and Nishan Rafi Havandjian. "Youth Media Imaginaries in Palestine: A Hermeneutic Exploration." *European Scientific Journal* 2 SE (December 8, 2013): 178–89.

Awad, Mira. "Where Do We Go from Here?" *Haaretz.com*, August 15, 2014. http://www.haaretz.com/opinion/.premium-1.610660.

Azoulay, Ariella. "Declaring the State of Israel: Declaring a State of War." *Critical Inquiry* 37, no. 2 (January 1, 2011): 265–85.

———. *The Civil Contract of Photography*. New York: Zone Books, 2008.

Azoulay, Ariella, and Adi Ophir. *The One-State Condition: Occupation and Democracy in Israel/Palestine*. Stanford, Calif.: Stanford University Press, 2013.

Baharir, Ruth Perl. "Israelis Launch Facebook Campaign Calling for 'Revenge' of Teens' Murders." *Haaretz.com*, July 2, 2014. http://www.haaretz.com/news/national/1.602661.

Barak, Oren, and Gabriel Sheffer. *Militarism and Israeli Society*. Bloomington: Indiana University Press, 2010.

"Bar-Ilan University Students Advocate for Israel During Operation Pillar of Defense." Bar-Ilan University, November 19, 2012. http://www1.biu.ac.il/index E.php?id=33&pt=20&pid=4&level=1&cPath=4&type=1&news=1774.

Barthes, Roland. *Camera Lucida: Reflections on Photography*, 1st American paperback ed. New York: Hill and Wang, 1982.

"Battleground Twitter (with Images, Tweets)." *Storify*, November 15, 2012. http://storify.com/ajstream/gaza-social-media-war.

Beinin, Joel. "Racism Is the Foundation of Israel's Operation Protective Edge." Stanford University Press Blog, July 30, 2014. http://stanfordpress.typepad.com/blog/2014/07/racism-is-the-foundation-of-israels-operation-protective-edge.html.

Beinin, Joel, and Rebecca L. Stein. "Histories and Futures of a Failed Peace." In *The Struggle for Sovereignty: Palestine and Israel, 1993–2005*, ed. Joel Beinin and Rebecca L. Stein, 1–26. Stanford, Calif.: Stanford University Press, 2006.

———, eds. *The Struggle for Sovereignty: Palestine and Israel, 1993–2005*. Stanford, Calif.: Stanford University Press, 2006.

Ben Israel, Dorri. "Eden Abergil—The Websurfers Version" [in Hebrew]. *Mizbala*, August 17, 2010. http://mizbala.com/?p=16584.

Ben-Ami, Yuval. "Mates [Heb. *Sachim*], They Don't Mind When Other People Suffer." *Everywhere*, August 16, 2010. http://yuvalbenami.blogspot.com/2010/08/sakhim-they-dont-mind-when-other-people.html.

Ben-Ari, Eyal. *Mastering Soldiers: Conflict, Emotions, and the Enemy in an Israeli Military Unit*. New York: Berghahn Books, 1998.

Ben-Ari, Eyal, and Edna Lomsky-Feder. "The Discourses of 'Psychology' and the 'Normalization' of War in the Israeli Context." In *Militarism and Israeli Society*, 280–303. Bloomington: Indiana University Press, 2010.

Ben-Eliezer, Uri. *The Making of Israeli Militarism*. Bloomington: Indiana University Press, 1998.

Ben-Israel, Adi. "Caught Red-Handed: A BBC Reporter Published a Picture of Dead Syrian girl, Presenting Her as an IDF Casuality in Gaza" [in Hebrew]. *Globes*, November 20, 2012. http://www.globes.co.il/news/article.aspx?fbdid=1000799711.

Benjamin, Walter. *The Work of Art in the Age of Mechanical Reproduction*. Scottsdale, Ariz.: Prism Key Press, 2010.

Bennett, Daniel. "Exploring the Impact of an Evolving War and Terror Blogosphere on Traditional Media Coverage of Conflict." *Media, War & Conflict* 6, no. 1 (April 1, 2013): 37–53.

Ben-Yishai, Ron. "IDF Must Put an End to Virtual Protest." *Ynet*, May 1, 2014. http://www.ynetnews.com/articles/0,7340,L-4515293,00.html.

Berenger, Ralph D. *Social Media Go to War: Rage, Rebellion and Revolution in the Age of Twitter*. Spokane, Wash.: Marquette Books, 2013.

———. *Cybermedia Go to War: Role of Converging Media During and After the 2003 Iraq War*. Spokane, Wash.: Marquette Books, 2006.

Berkman, Fran. "Russia Blocks Pro-Ukraine Groups on Social Media." *Mashable*, March 3, 2014. http://mashable.com/2014/03/03/russia-ukraine-internet/.

Bi'our, Haim, and Hila Weisburg. "'Death to Arabs,' '13 Soldiers Dead—Lets Have More' Should Employees Get Fired because of Facebook?" [in Hebrew]. *The Marker*, July 30, 2014, http://www.themarker.com/career/1.2390429.

Blau, Uri. "Israeli Troops Humiliate Palestinians—and Put It on YouTube." *Haaretz.com*, June 19, 2009. http://www.haaretz.com/news/israeli-troops-hum iliate-palestinians-and-put-it-on-youtube-1.278442.

Blecher, Robert. "Living on the Edge." *Middle East Resesearch and Information Project*, Winter 2002. http://www.merip.org/mer/mer225/living-edge.

Blumenthal, Max. "IDF Releases Apparently Doctored Flotilla Audio: Press Reports As Fact." Max Blumenthal, June 4, 2010. http://maxblumenthal.com /2010/06/idf-releases-apparently-doctored-audio-press-reports-as-fact/.

Boler, Megan. *Digital Media and Democracy: Tactics in Hard Times*. Cambridge, Mass.: MIT Press, 2008.

boyd, danah. *It's Complicated: The Social Lives of Networked Teens*. New Haven, Conn., and London: Yale University Press, 2014.

boyd, danah, Scott Golder, and Gilad Lotan. "Tweet, Tweet, Retweet: Conversational Aspects of Retweeting on Twitter." In *Proceedings of the 2010 43rd Hawaii International Conference on System Sciences*, 1–10. HICSS '10. Washington, D.C.: IEEE Computer Society, 2010.

Breaking the Silence. *Our Harsh Logic: Israeli Soldiers' Testimonies from the Occupied Territories, 2000–2010*. New York: Henry Holt, 2012.

"Breaking the Silence: Israeli Soldiers Talk about the Occupied Territories," n.d. http://www.breakingthesilence.org.il/.

Breiner, Yehoshua. "Humiliating Palestinians on FaceBook: The Border Police Is Also Into It" [in Hebrew]. *Walla! News*, August 18, 2010. http://news.walla .co.il/?w=/1/1723422.

Brownfield-Stein, Chava. *Fantasy of the State, Photographs of IDF Female Soldiers, and the Eroticization of Civil Militarism in Israel* [in Hebrew]. Tel Aviv: Resling, 2012.

———. "Visual Representations of IDF Women Soldiers and 'Civil-Militarism' in Israel." In *Militarism and Israeli Society*, ed. Gabriel Sheffer and Oren Barak. Bloomington: Indiana University Press, 2010.

Brumer, David. "Conversations: What 'Ordinary' Israelis Think About Ha'Matzav' or 'The Situation.'" Accessed June 25, 2014. http://brumspeak.blog spot.co.uk/2007/09/conversations-with-israelis-what.html.

"B'Tselem Questions Israeli Account of Attack—1 Jan 09, 2009." http://www .youtube.com/watch?v=xBYkrGIFnvI&feature=youtube_gdata_player.

Butler, Judith. *Frames of War: When Is Life Grievable?* Reprint ed. London; New York: Verso, 2010.

Byers, David. "Gaza: Secondary War Being Fought on the Internet." *The Times* (London), December 31, 2008, sec. Technology. http://www.thetimes.co.uk/tto/technology/article1859190.ece.

Caldwell, William B., Anton Menning, and Dennis M. Murphy. "Learning to Leverage New Media: The Israeli Defense Forces in Recent Conflicts." *Military Review*, 2009. General OneFile.

"Capt. Barak Raz Responds to Shameful Facebook Photos Uploaded by Discharged IDF Soldier," 2010. http://www.youtube.com/watch?v=aQFAvv8Htrk&feature=youtube_gdata_player.

Carafano, James Jay. *Wiki at War: Conflict in a Socially Networked World.* College Station, Tex.: Texas A&M University Press, 2012.

Carr, David. "At Front Lines, Bearing Witness in Real Time," *The New York Times*, July 27, 2014. http://www.nytimes.com/2014/07/28/business/media/at-front-lines-bearing-witness-in-real-time.html.

Chancey, Diana L. "*New Media: The Key to Influence in Irregular Warfare,*" Naval War College, May 20, 2013. http://oai.dtic.mil/oai/oai?verb=getRecord&metadataPrefix=html&identifier=ADA583349.

"Checkdesk." Accessed February 3, 2014. http://checkdesk.org/.

"Checkdesk: A New Approach to Fact-Checking Citizen Media of the Arab Spring." *Meedan.org.* Accessed February 3, 2014. http://meedan.org/2012/03/verification-citizen-journalism-middle-east-uprisings/.

Chen, Adrian. "The Laborers Who Keep Dick Pics and Beheadings Out of Your Facebook Feed." *Wired*, October 23, 2014. http://www.wired.com/2014/10/content-moderation.

"Clarification/Correction Regarding Audio Transmission Between Israeli Navy and Flotilla on 31 May 2010, Posted on 5 June 2010." IDF Blog: The Official Blog of the Israel Defense Forces, June 5, 2010.http://docstalk.blogspot.co.uk/2010/06/clarificationcorrection-regarding-audio.html.

Clough, Patricia. "War by Other Means: What Difference Does the Graphic(s) Make." In *Digital Cultures and The Politics of Emotions*, ed. Adi Kuntsman and Athina Karatzogianni. Houndmills, Basingstoke, Hampshire; New York: Palgrave Macmillan, 2012.

Cohen, Akiba A., Dafna Lemish, and Amit Schejter. *The Wonder Phone in the Land of Miracles: Mobile Telephony in Israel.* Cresskill, N.J.: Hampton Press, 2008.

Cohen, Gili. "Israeli Soldier Aims Gun at Teen in Video Clip." *Haaretz.com*, April 29, 2014. http://www.haaretz.com/news/diplomacy-defense/.premium-1.587922.

———. "A New Directive Will Impose Restrictions on IDF Soldiers' Use of

Facebook" [in Hebrew]. *Haaretz.com*, June 5, 2013. http://www.haaretz.co.il/news/politics/.premium-1.2038947.

Cohen, Noam. "In Gaza Conflict, Fighting with Weapons and Postings on Twitter." *The New York Times*, November 21, 2012, sec. World / Middle East. http://www.nytimes.com/2012/11/22/world/middleeast/in-gaza-conflict-fighting-with-weapons-and-postings-on-twitter.html.

Cook, Jonathan. "Israel's Gaza Backlash Targets Arab Minority." *Middle East Eye*, July 30, 2014. http://www.middleeasteye.net/news/israel-s-gaza-backlash-targets-arab-minority-483153084.

———. "Cultures of Hate: Israelis, Not Palestinians, Excel at Vengeance." *Global Research*, July 9, 2014. http://www.globalresearch.ca/cul tures-of-hate-israelis-not-palestinians-excel-at-vengeance/5390590?utm_source=rss&utm_medium=rss&utm_campaign=cultures-of-hate-israelis-not-palestinians-excel-at-vengeance.

———. "Palestinian Social Media Campaigns Unlike Egyptian, Tunisian Counterparts." *Washington Report on Middle East Affairs*, 2011. Academic OneFile.

Cooper, Stephen. "A Concise History of the Fauxtography Blogstorm in the 2006 Lebanon War." Communications Faculty Research, July 1, 2007. http://mds.marshall.edu/communications_faculty/3.

Danan, Lizette. "The Unbearable Lightness of Google+ Enter" [in Hebrew]. *Mako*, August 18, 2010. http://www.mako.co.il/nexter-archive/Article-690e9e4a0148a21006.htm.

Daniel, Lars E. *Digital Forensics for Legal Professionals: Understanding Digital Evidence from the Warrant to the Courtroom*. Waltham, Mass.: Syngress/Elsevier, 2011.

Darcy, Shane, and John Reynolds. "'Otherwise Occupied': The Status of the Gaza Strip from the Perspective of International Humanitarian Law." *Journal of Conflict and Security Law*, August 11, 2010.

Dawn, Talia. "Soldier from Facebook Captured the World's Headlines" [in Hebrew]. *Walla! News*, August 17, 2010. http://news.walla.co.il/?w=/2/1722735.

"A Dead Man Came to Life in Gaza" [in Hebrew]. *The Butterfly Effect*, November 16, 2012. http://healworlds.blogspot.co.il/2012/11/a-dead-man-came-to-life-in-gaza.html.

Denning, Dorothy E. "Information Technology and Security." In *Grave New World: Security Challenges in the 21st Century*, ed. Michael E. Brown, 91–112. Washington, D.C.: Georgetown University Press, 2003.

Derfner, Larry. "Ceasefire Tells the World: Gaza Still Under Israeli Occupation." *+972 Magazine*, November 23, 2012. Accessed June 25, 2014. http://972mag.com/ceasefire-tells-the-world-gaza-still-under-israeli-occupation/60669/.

Derfner, Larry. "On the Al-Dura Affair: Israel Officially Drank the Kool Aid." *+972 Magazine*, May 22, 2013. http://972mag.com/on-the-al-dura-affair-israel -officially-drank-the-kool-aid/71812/.

Derian, James Der. *Virtuous War: Mapping the Military-Industrial-Media-Entertainment-Network*. New York: Routledge, 2009.

Derrida, Jacques. *Archive Fever: A Freudian Impression*. Chicago: University of Chicago Press, 1998.

Diamond, Larry Jay, and Marc F. Plattner, eds. *Liberation Technology: Social Media and the Struggle for Democracy*. Baltimore: Johns Hopkins University Press, 2012.

"Digital Photography Experts Confirm the Integrity of Paul Hansens's Image Files." World Press Photo, May 14, 2013. http://www.worldpressphoto.org/news/ digital-photography-experts-confirm-integrity-paul-hansen-image-files.

Dijk, Jan van, and Kenneth L. Hacker, eds. *Digital Democracy: Issues of Theory and Practice*. London; Thousand Oaks, Calif.: Sage, 2000.

Doherty, Benjamin. "War Sporno: How the Israeli Army Uses Sex and Instagram to Sell Its Racism and Violence." *The Electronic Intifada*, December 26, 2012. http://electronicintifada.net/blogs/benjamin-doherty/war-sporno-how -israeli-army-uses-sex-and-instagram-sell-its-racism-and.

Doron, Gideon, and Azi Lev-On. *New Media, Politics and Society in Israel*. London; New York: Routledge, 2012.

Downey, Anthony, ed. *Uncommon Grounds: New Media and Critical Practices in the Middle East and North Africa*. London: I.B. Taurus, 2014.

Dyer-Witheford, Nick, and Greig De Peuter. *Games of Empire: Global Capitalism and Video Games*. Minneapolis: University of Minnesota Press, 2009.

Economist Intelligence Unit, "Digital Economy Rankings 2010: Beyond E-Readiness." *The Economist*, June 2010. http://graphics.eiu.com/upload/EIU _Digital_economy_rankings_2010_FINAL_WEB.pdf.

"Eden Abergil and Handcuffed Palestinians—Is Facebook to Blame?" [in Hebrew]. *Holes in the Net*, August 16, 2010. http://www.holesinthenet.co.il/holes inthenet-media-story-23348.

"Eden Abergil, Meet the Internet" [in Hebrew]. *Room 404*. Accessed November 1, 2010. http://room404.net/?p=33326.

"Eden Abergil, Poses with Bound Palestinians, Does Not Understand What Is Wrong" [in Hebrew]. *Haaretz.com*, August 17, 2010. http://www.haaretz.co .il/news/education/1.1217056.

"Eden Abergil, Racism and Patriarchy" [in Hebrew]. *Black-Purple*, August 17, 2010. http://bidyke.wordpress.com.

"Eden Abergil—Support Campaign." *Twibbon*. Accessed August 20, 2013. http://twibbon.com/Support/Eden-Abergil.

Eglash, Ruth. "#IsraelUnderFire from Gaza Plays out on Twitter." *The Jerusalem Post*, March 11, 2011. http://www.jpost.com/Defense/IsraelUnderFire-from -Gaza-plays-out-on-Twitter.

Eichorn, Kate. "Archival Genres: Gathering Texts and Reading Spaces." *Invisible Culture* 12, 2008. http://www.rochester.edu/in_visible_culture/Issue_12/eich horn/eichhorn.pdf.

Elbaz, Rotem. "The War for 'Likes': Pillar of Defense on the Internet" [in Hebrew]. *Maamul*, November 19, 2012. http://maamul.sapir.ac.il/2012/11/6965/.

el-Nawawy, Mohammed, and Sahar Khamis. *Egyptian Revolution 2.0: Political Blogging, Civic Engagement, and Citizen Journalism*. New York: Palgrave Macmillan, 2013.

Eördögh, Fruzsina. "Instagram Photos of Smiling Soldiers Show Israel Is Now Losing Its Gaza Social Media War." *Future Tense*, November 16, 2012. http:// www.slate.com/blogs/future_tense/2012/11/16/pillarofdefense_vs_gazaunder attack_idf_is_now_losing_its_social_media_war.html.

"Even on Independence Day: Protest Against the Restraint Policy Continues" [in Hebrew]. *0404 Blog*, June 5, 2014. http://0404.co.il/post/7350.

Everard, Jerry. *Virtual States: The Internet and the Boundaries of the Nation-State*. New York: Routledge, 2000.

"Ex-Soldier Presents Cuffed Palestinian Friends." *Ynet*, August 16, 2010. http:// www.ynetnews.com/articles/0,7340,L-3937459,00.html.

Fabian, Johannes. *Time and the Other: How Anthropology Makes Its Object*. New York: Columbia University Press, 2002.

"'Facebook Photos of Soldiers Posing with Bound Palestinians Are the Norm.'" *Haaretz.com*, August 17, 2010. http://www.haaretz.com/news/diplomacy-de fense/facebook-photos-of-soldiers-posing-with-bound-palestinians-are-the -norm-1.308582.

Fahmy, Shahira, and Britain Eakin. "High Drama on the High Seas: Peace Versus War Journalism Framing of an Israeli/Palestinian-Related Incident." *International Communication Gazette* 76, no. 1 (February 1, 2014): 86–105.

"Famous Internet Hoaxes." *The Telegraph*, June 13, 2011, sec. Internet. http://www .telegraph.co.uk/technology/internet/8571780/Famous-internet-hoaxes.html.

"Fan Photos from We Are All with Eden Abergil." Facebook. Accessed August 20, 2010. Link no longer exists.

Fausing, Bent. "Selfies and the Search for Recognition: See for Your Selfie." *Academia.edu*. Accessed June 26, 2014. https://www.academia.edu/4418191/ Selfies_and_the_Search_for_Recognition._See_for_your_Selfie.

Feiler, Boaz, and Netanel Schmulovitch. "Pictures with a Handcuffed Palestinian: 'I Took Care of the Detainees'" [in Hebrew]. *Ynet*, August 17, 2010. http://www.ynet.co.il/articles/0,7340,L-3937757,00.html.

"Female IDF Soldiers Punished for Racy Photos." *Ynet*, June 13, 2013. http://www.ynetnews.com/articles/0,7340,L-4387423,00.html.

Ferreday, Debra. "Affect, Fantasy and Digital Cultures." In *Digital Cultures and the Politics of Emotions: Feelings, Affect and Technological Change*, ed. Adi Kuntsman and Athina Karatzogianni. Houndmills, Basingstoke, Hampshire; New York: Palgrave Macmillan, 2012.

Ferreday, Debra, and Adi Kuntsman. "Introduction: Haunted Futurities." *Borderlands* 10, no. 2 (2011).

Fine, Yonatan. "On Eden Aberjil and the Bite of the Man" [in Hebrew]. *The Shocking True Story Of . . .* , August 17, 2010. http://www.hahem.co.il/trueand shocking/?p=1073%20%E2%80%93%20%22On%20Eden%20Aberjil%20 and%20the%20bite%20of%20the%20Man%22.

"First Twitter War Declaration? Israel Announces Gaza Operation on Social Media Site." *RT*, November 14, 2012. http://rt.com/news/first-israel-gaza-idf-706/.

Fiske, Gavriel. "Israelis Love Their Touch Screens." *The Times of Israel*. Accessed September 29, 2013. http://www.timesofisrael.com/israelis-love-their-touch -screens/.

Flintoff, Corey. "Gaza Conflict Plays Out Online Through Social Media." *NPR. org*, January 6, 2009. http://www.npr.org/templates/story/story.php?storyId= 99043190.

"Flotilla For Palestine." Facebook. Accessed August 10, 2013. https://www.face book.com/pages/Flotilla-For-Palestine/108527149182640.

Flower, Kevin. "Facebook Page Supporting Palestinian Intifada Pulled down." CNN, March 29, 2011. http://www.cnn.com/2011/WORLD/meast/03/29/ palestinian.facebook/index.html?_s=PM:WORLD.

"Former-IDF Censor: I Also Have Revealing Photos." *Ynet*, June 5, 2013. http:// www.ynetnews.com/articles/0,7340,L-4388592,00.html.

"47 Years of Temporary Occupation." *B'Tselem*, n.d. Accessed September 19, 2014. http://www.btselem.org/publications/47_year_long_temporary_occupation.

"Freegaza." Accessed August 10, 2013. http://www.freegaza.org/.

"From Cast Lead to Pillar of Defense: How the IDF Has Learnt to Communicate War in Gaza Online." *Frontline Club*, November 21, 2012. http:// www.frontlineclub.com/from-cast-lead-to-pillar-of-defense-how-the-idf-has -learnt-to-communicate-war-in-gaza-online/.

Gabbay, Shoshana. "Whose Blindfold Is This?" [in Hebrew]. *HaOkets*, August 19, 2010. http://www.haokets.org.

Galon, Zehava. "Eden Aberjil Also Breaks the Silence" [in Hebrew]. *Israel Hayom*, August 8, 2010. http://www.israelhayom.co.il/site/newsletter_opinion.php?id =4374.

"Ganav Statusim" (Cool Statuses; in Hebrew). Facebook. Accessed November 11, 2012. https://www.facebook.com/photo.php?fbid=296365783814288&set=a.12 8966077220927.24925.121960967921438&type=1&permPage=1.

Garde-Hansen, Joanne, Andrew Hoskins, and Anna Reading. *Save As . . . Digital Memories*. Basingstoke, U.K.; New York: Palgrave School, Print UK, 2009.

Gavriely-Nuri, Dalia. *The Normalization of War in Israeli Discourse, 1967–2008*. Lanham, Md.: Rowman & Littlefield, 2012.

Gibson, Rachel Kay, Andrea Römmele, and Stephen Ward. *Electronic Democracy: Mobilisation, Organisation and Participation via New ICTs*. London; New York: Routledge, 2004.

Gilinsky, Jaron. "How Social Media War Was Waged in Gaza-Israel Conflict." PBS: *Mediashift*, February 13, 2009. http://www.pbs.org/mediashift/2009/02/how-social-media-war-was-waged-in-gaza-israel-conflict044/.

Gitelman, Lisa. *Always Already New: Media, History and the Data of Culture*. Cambridge, Mass.; London: MIT Press, 2008.

Glickman, Aviad. "'Facebook Soldier' Won't Be Probed." *Ynet*, June 16, 2011. http://www.ynetnews.com/articles/0,7340,L-4083229,00.html.

Golan, Boaz. "Senior Figure in the IDF on the Protests Which Began on 0404: 'This Is a Digital Tsunami'" [in Hebrew]. Blog *0404*, April 30, 2014. http://0404 .co.il/post/7007.

———. "IDF Soldiers Started a Protest Against a Suspended Soldier Who Pointed a Weapon at an Arab in Hebron" [in Hebrew]. Blog *0404*, April 29, 2014. http://www.0404.co.il/post/6929.

Golden, Deborah. "Fear, Politics and Children: Israeli-Jewish and Israeli-Palestinian Preschool Teachers Talk About Political Violence." *Etnofoor* 21, no. 2 (2009): 77–95.

———. "Childhood as Protected Space? Vulnerable Bodies in an Israeli Kindergarten." *Ethnos* 70, no. 1 (March 1, 2005): 79–100.

"A Good Picture Is Worth a Thousand Words?" [in Hebrew]. *Fake You*. http://bit.ly/16rRjkV. Accessed August 17, 2013.

Gor, Haggith. "Education for War in Israel: Preparing Children to Accept War as a Natural Factor of Life." In *Education as an Enforcement: The Militarization and Corporatization of Schools*, ed. Ken Saltman and David Gabbard. New York: Routledge, 2003, 209–217.

Gordon, Neve. "Israel's Emergence as a Homeland Security Capital." In *Surveil-*

lance and Control in Israel/Palestine: Population, Territory and Power, ed. Elia Zureik. New York: Routledge, 2010.

———. *The Political Economy of Israel's Homeland Security Industry*. The Surveillance Project, Queens University, April 2009.

———. *Israel's Occupation*. Berkeley: University of California Press, 2008.

Gregory, Paul Roderick. "Inside Putin's Campaign of Social Media Trolling and Faked Ukrainian Crimes." *Forbes*, May 11, 2014. http://www.forbes.com/sites/paulroderickgregory/2014/05/11/inside-putins-campaign-of-social-media-trolling-and-faked-ukrainian-crimes/.

Gregory, Sam. "Images of Horror: Whose Roles and What Responsibility?" *Witness Blog*, September 18, 2014. http://blog.witness.org/2014/09/sharing-images-horror-roles-responsibilities.

———. "Cameras Everywhere: Ubiquitous Video Documentation of Human Rights, New Forms of Video Advocacy, and Considerations of Safety, Security, Dignity and Consent." *Journal of Human Rights Practice* 2, no. 2 (July 1, 2010): 191–207. doi:10.1093/jhuman/huq002.

Grimland, Guy. "Israeli PR's Hottest Merchandise—Eden Abergil" [in Hebrew]. *The Marker*, August 16, 2010. http://www.themarker.com/technation/1.582247.

Grimland, Guy, Zvi Zrahiya, and Matan Mittelman. "Israel Launches National Cyber Command—Israel News | Haaretz." *Haaretz.com*, May 19, 2011. http://www.haaretz.com/business/israel-launches-national-cyber-command-1.362656.

Grinberg, Lev Luis. "The J14 Resistance Mo(ve)ment: The Israeli Mix of Tahrir Square and Puerta Del Sol." *Current Sociology* 61, no. 4 (July 1, 2013): 491–509.

Guarav, Mishra. "War 2.0, Propaganda 2.0 or Public Diplomacy 2.0: The Role of Internet and Mobile in Israel's Gaza Strip Bombing." *Gauravonomics Blog*, January 3, 2009. http://web.archive.org/web/20090115075953/http://www.gauravonomics.com/blog/war-20-israel-uses-internet-and-mobile-propaganda-in-gaza-strip-bombing/.

Gurvitz, Yossi. "Lt. Aberjeel's Sense of Humor." *Wish You Orwell*, August 16, 2010. http://web.archive.org/web/20100819230803/http://ygurvitz.net/?p=31.

Hague, Barry N., and Brian Loader, eds. *Digital Democracy: Discourse and Decision Making in the Information Age*. London; New York: Routledge, 1999.

Hajjar, Lisa. "Is Gaza Still Occupied and Why Does It Matter?" *Jadaliyya*, July 14, 2014. http://www.jadaliyya.com/pages/index/8807/is-gaza-still-occupied-and-why-does-it-matter.

Halevi, Yossi Klein. *At the Entrance to the Garden of Eden: A Jew's Search for Hope with Christians and Muslims in the Holy Land.* Updated edition. New York: HarperPerennial, 2002.

Hammami, Rema, and Salim Tamari. "Anatomy of Another Rebellion." *Middle East Report*, Winter 2000. http://www.merip.org/mer/mer217/anatomy -another-rebellion.

Hardy, Mat. "#IDF v #Hamas: The New Gaza War in 140 Characters or Less." *The Conversation*, November 15, 2012. http://theconversation.com/ idf-v-hamas-the-new-gaza-war-in-140-characters-or-less-10762.

Harel, Amos, and Gili Cohen. "The IDF's First Digital Rebellion" [in Hebrew]. *Haaretz.com*, April 30, 2014. http://www.haaretz.co.il/news/politics/.premium -1.2309469.

Harkov, Lahav. "Hamas Co-Opts Photos of Injured Syrians." *The Jerusalem Post*, November 18, 2012. http://www.jpost.com/Features/In-Thespotlight/Hamas -co-opts-photos-of-injured-Syrians.

———. "Facebook Flooded with Photos of Detainees." *The Jerusalem Post*, August 17, 2010. http://www.jpost.com/Israel/Facebook-flooded-with-photos-of -detainees.

———. "'IDF Facebook Photos Are the Norm.'" *The Jerusalem Post*, August 17, 2010. http://www.jpost.com/Israel/IDF-Facebook-photos-are-the-norm.

Harris, Rachel S., and Ranen Omer-Sherman, eds. *Narratives of Dissent: War in Contemporary Israeli Arts and Culture.* Detroit: Wayne State University Press, 2012.

Hassine, Tsila. Interview by Rebecca L. Stein, May 2013.

Hasson, Nir. "Murder of Palestinian Teen Was No 'Honor Killing,' Says His Family." *Haaretz.com*, July 6, 2014. http://www.haaretz.com/news/diplomacy -defense/.premium-1.602736.

Heemsbergen, Luke Justin, and Simon Lindgren. "The Power of Precision Air Strikes and Social Media Feeds in the 2012 Israel–Hamas Conflict: 'Targeting Transparency.'" *Australian Journal of International Affairs* 68, no. 5 (2014): 569–91.

Hijazi-Omari, Hiyam, and Rivka Ribak. "Playing with Fire: On the Domestication of the Mobile Phone Among Palestinian Teenage Girls in Israel." *Information, Communication & Society* 11, no. 2 (2008): 149–66.

Hindman, Matthew Scott. *The Myth of Digital Democracy.* Princeton, N.J.: Princeton University Press, 2009.

Hjorth, Larissa, and Sarah Pink. "New Visualities and the Digital Wayfarer: Reconceptualizing Camera Phone Photography and Locative Media." *Mobile Media & Communication* 2, no. 1 (January 1, 2014): 40–57.

Hodge, Nathan. "YouTube, Twitter: Weapons in Israel's Info War." *Wired*, December 30, 2008. http://www.wired.com/2008/12/israels-info-wa/.

Hoffman, Tzahi. "57% of Israelis Have Smartphones" [in Hebrew]. *Globes*, October 6, 2013. http://www.globes.co.il/en/article-1000851195.

Hollander, Ricki. "Updated: A Reprise: Media Photo Manipulation." *Committee for Accuracy in Middle East Reporting in America*, August 9, 2006. http://www.camera.org/index.asp?x_context=2&x_outlet=2&x_article=1175.

Horovitz, David. "Comment: A Scandalous Saga of Withheld Film." *The Jerusalem Post*, June 2, 2010. http://www.jpost.com/Israel/Comment-A-scandalous-saga-of-withheld-film.

Hoskins, Andrew, and Ben O'Loughlin. *War and Media: The Emergence of Diffused War*. Cambridge, U.K.; Malden, Mass.: Polity Press, 2010.

"Hotline, That's What I Have?" [in Hebrew]. *Room 404*, July 8, 2014. http://room404.net/?p=63534.

"How Researchers Use Social Media to Map the Conflict in Syria." *Forbes*. Accessed May 27, 2014. http://www.forbes.com/sites/federicoguerrini/2014/04/15/how-researchers-use-social-media-to-map-armed-forces-in-syria/.

"How the IDF Fell Off the Social Media Bandwagon." *Frontline Club*, February 25, 2009. http://www.frontlineclub.com/the_problems_with_the_israeli_defence_forces_social_media_campaign/.

Howard, Philip N., and Hussain, Muzammil M. *Democracy's Fourth Wave?: Digital Media and the Arab Spring*. New York: Oxford University Press, 2013.

"I Am Ashamed of the Picture and Regret It" [in Hebrew]. *Mako*, July 7, 2013. http://www.mako.co.il/entertainment-celebs/local/Article-30441b88b09bf31006.htm&Partner=facebook_comments?fb_comment_id=fbc_630781933600309_7269171_631272380217931#f32776f18c.

"I Understood What's Wrong, I Apologized to Those Who Were Hurt" [in Hebrew]. *Nana10*, August 17, 2010. http://news.nana10.co.il/Article/?ArticleID=739706.

"IDF Broadcasts Hizbullah's Dead on Al-Manar." *Ynet*, August 8, 2006. http://www.ynetnews.com/articles/0,7340,L-3288442,00.html.

"IDF Plans Social Media Clampdown for Soldiers." *The Times of Israel*, June 7, 2013. http://www.timesofisrael.com/idf-plans-social-media-clampdown-for-soldiers/.

"IDF Soldier Posts Images of Blindfolded Palestinians on Facebook, from 'Best Time of My Life.'" *Haaretz.com*, August 16, 2010. http://www.haaretz.com/news/national/idf-soldier-posts-images-of-blindfolded-palestinians-on-facebook-from-best-time-of-my-life-1.308402.

"IHH Insani Yardim Vakfi." *Livestream*. Accessed August 10, 2013. http://www
.livestream.com/insaniyardim.

"Iran Does It Again: Faked Missile Reminiscent of 'Green Helmet Guy' and Other
Staged News Events." The Israel Project, June 10, 2008. http://www.theisrael
project.org/site/c.hsJPKoPIJpH/b.672631/apps/s/content.asp?ct=5996603.

"Israel Defense Forces." YouTube. Accessed August 10, 2013. http://www.you
tube.com/user/idfnadesk.

"Israel en España." Facebook. Accessed November 20, 2012. https://www.facebook
.com/photo.php?fbid=467170993324452&set=a.401254089916143.82837.139691
532739068&type=1&relevant_count=1.

"Israel Ranks 7 in Global Broadband Penetration." *Ynet*. Accessed October 4, 2013.
http://www.ynetnews.com/articles/0,7340,L-3734564,00.html.

"Israel to Pay Students to Defend It Online." *USA Today*, August 14, 2013. http://
www.usatoday.com/story/news/world/2013/08/14/israel-students-social
-media/2651715/.

"Israel Under Fire." Facebook. Accessed August 10, 2013. https://www.facebook
.com/IsraelUnderFireLive.

"Israel Under Fire." Facebook. Accessed November 22, 2012. https://www.face
book.com/photo.php?fbid=389568781119995&set=a.270022616407946.61972
.269844029759138&type=1&relevant_count=1.

"Israel Under Fire." Facebook. Accessed November 21, 2012. https://www.face
book.com/photo.php?fbid=390443734365833&set=a.270022616407946.6197
2.269844029759138&type=1&relevant_count=1.

"Israel Under Fire." Facebook. Accessed November 20, 2012. https://www.face
book.com/photo.php?fbid=390061411070732&set=a.270022616407946.6197
2.269844029759138&type=1&relevant_count=1.

"Israel Under Fire." Israel Defense Forces. Accessed August 16, 2013. http://www
.idfblog.com/2012/11/21/israel-under-fire-largest-israeli-cities-under-attack/.

"Israeli Justice." Facebook. Accessed August 1, 2014. https://www.facebook.com/
Israelijustice?sk=photos_stream.

"Israeli-Arab Party Blames 'Occupation' for Violence After Kidnapped Teens
Found Dead." *www.JPost.com*. Accessed July 2, 2014. http://www.jpost.com/
Operation-Brothers-Keeper/Israeli-Arab-party-blames-occupation-for-vio
lence-after-kidnapped-teens-found-dead-361244.

Israeli Ministry of Tourism. "Communications in Israel." www.goisrael.com. Accessed August 1, 2014. http://www.goisrael.com/Tourism_Eng/Tourist%20
Information/Planning%20your%20trip/Pages/Communications.aspx.

"Israelis Do Not Join the Radical Leftist Group 'We Are All with Eden Abergil.'"
Facebook, n.d. The Facebook page has been removed.

"Israel's Court Defeats Film Ban." BBC, August 31, 2004, sec. Entertainment. http://news.bbc.co.uk/2/hi/entertainment/3613658.stm.

Issacharoff, Avi, Yuval Azoulay, Anshel Pfeffer, and Jack Khoury. "Protest Flotilla Begins to Move Toward Gaza" [in Hebrew]. *Haaretz.com*, May 30, 2010. http://www.haaretz.co.il/news/politics/1.1204225.

Isseroff, Ami. "The Palestine Nakba Controversy." *Zionism-Israel.com*, 2008. http://zionism-israel.com/his/Palestine_Nakba.htm.

"Issue 4: War, Conflict and Commemoration in the Age of Digital Reproduction." *Digital Icons*, 2014. http://www.digitalicons.org/issue04.

Ivry, Tsipy. *Embodying Culture: Pregnancy in Japan and Israel.* New Brunswick, N.J.: Rutgers University Press, 2010.

Jenin: IDF Military Operations. Human Rights Watch, May 2002. http://www.hrw.org/reports/2002/israel3/israel0502-01.htm#P49_1774.

Johnson, Charles. "Reuters Doctoring Photos from Beirut?" Little Green Footballs, August 5, 2006. http://littlegreenfootballs.com/weblog/?entry=21956_Reuters_Doctoring_Photos_from_Beirut&only.

Junka-Aikio, Laura. "Late Modern Subjects of Colonial Occupation: Mobile Phones and the Rise of Neoliberalism in Palestine." *New Formations*, no. 75 (2012): 99–121.

Kalb, Marvin, and Carol Saivetz. "The Israeli-Hezbollah War of 2006: The Media as a Weapon in Asymmetrical Conflict." *The Harvard International Journal of Press/Politics* 12, no. 3 (July 1, 2007): 43–66.

Kanaaneh, Rhoda Ann. *Surrounded: Palestinian Soldiers in the Israeli Military.* Stanford, Calif.: Stanford University Press, 2009.

Kantrowitz, Alex. "The United States' Social Media Plan to Keep Syria's Chemical Weapons Safe." *Forbes*, February 10, 2013. http://www.forbes.com/sites/alexkantrowitz/2013/02/10/individual-intervention-u-s-connecting-with-syrian-officers-on-social-media-in-attempt-to-keep-chemical-weapons-safe/.

Kaplan, Caren. "The Biopolitics of Technoculture in the Mumbai Attacks." *Theory, Culture and Society* 26, no. 7-8 (December 2009): 301–13.

Kaplan, Danny. *Brothers and Others in Arms: The Making of Love and War in Israeli Combat Units.* New York: Southern Tier Editions/Harrington Park Press, 2003.

Karatzogianni, Athina. "Introduction." In *Cyberconflict and Global Politics*, ed. Athina Karatzogianni. London; New York: Routledge, 2009.

———. *The Politics of Cyberconflict.* London; New York: Routledge, 2006.

Kershner, Isabel. "6 Israelis Held Over the Killing of Palestinian." *The New York Times*, July 6, 2014. http://www.nytimes.com/2014/07/07/world/middleeast/israel-palestinians-muhammad-abu-khdeir.html.

Khalili, Laleh. "Virtual Nation: Palestinian Cyberculture in Lebanese Camps." In *Palestine, Israel, and the Politics of Popular Culture*, ed. Rebecca L. Stein and Ted Swedenburg, 126–49. Durham, N.C.: Duke University Press, 2005.

Kimmerling, Baruch. *The Invention and Decline of Israeliness: State, Society, and the Military*. Berkeley: University of California Press, 2001.

———. "Militarism in Israeli Society." *Theory and Criticism*, no. 4 (1993): 124.

Kling, Amit. "Days of Our Lives" [in Hebrew]. *Nana10*, August 17, 2010. http://bidur.nana10.co.il/Article/?ArticleID=739685.

Kozaryn, Linda D. "Tactical Internet Key to Digital Battlefield." U.S. Department of Defense, April 6, 2000. http://www.defense.gov/News/NewsArticle.aspx?ID=45084.

Kuntsman, Adi. "Anti-Humanitarian Citizenship: Coloniality, War and Necropolitics in Israel/Palestine." Biopolitics and Humanitarian Citizenship conference, The University of Manchester, United Kingdom, 2012.

———. "Digital Archives of Feelings and Their Haunted Futures." *Borderlands* 10, no. 2 (2011).

———. "Webs of Hate in Diasporic Cyberspaces: The Gaza War in the Russian-Language Blogosphere." *Media, War & Conflict* 3, no. 3 (December 1, 2010): 299–313.

———. *Figurations of Violence and Belonging: Queerness, Migranthood and Nationalism in Cyberspace and Beyond*. New York: Peter Lang, 2009.

———. "The Soldier and the Terrorist: Sexy Nationalism, Queer Violence." *Sexualities* 11, no. 1–2 (February 1, 2008): 142–70.

———. "Written in Blood." *Feminist Media Studies* 8, no. 3 (2008): 267–83.

Kuntsman, Adi, and Rebecca L. Stein. "Digital Suspicion, Politics, and the Middle East," *Critical Inquiry*, 2011. http://criticalinquiry.uchicago.edu/digital_suspicion_politics_and_the_middle_east.

———. "Another War Zone." *Middle East Report*, September 2010. http://www.merip.org/mero/interventions/another-war-zone.

Lagerquist, Peter. "Shooting Gaza: Photographers, Photographs, and the Unbearable Lightness of War." *Journal of Palestine Studies* 38, no. 3 (April 1, 2009): 86–92.

Landau, Idan. "Israel Gives Up White Phosphorus, Because 'It Doesn't Photograph Well'." *+972 Magazine*, April 28, 2013. http://972mag.com/israel-gives-up-white-phosphorus-because-it-doesnt-photograph-well/70063/.

Landes, Richard. "The Corruption of the Media." *EU Referendum*, August 15, 2006. http://eureferendum.blogspot.com/2006/08/corruption-of-media.html.

———. "Post on Washington Post Removed." *The Augean Stables*, August 6, 2006. http://www.theaugeanstables.com/2006/08/06/post-on-washington-post-removed/.

Lapide, Joshua. "'Jewish Nationalism' Behind Young Palestinian's Death." *Asia News*, July 7, 2014. http://www.asianews.it/news-en/%27Jewish-nationalism %27-behind-young-Palestinian%27s-death-31557.html.

Lappin, Yaakov. "AP Beirut Photo Faces Questions." *Ynet*, August 11, 2006. http://web.archive.org/web/20060811152130/http://www.ynetnews.com/ articles/0,7340,L-3288406,00.html.

———. "New York Times 'Used Fraudulent Photo.'" *Ynet*, August 11, 2006. http://web.archive.org/web/20060811160801/http://www.ynetnews.com/ articles/0,7340,L-3288887,00.html.

———. "Israeli War Deaths Go Largely Unnoticed." *Ynet*, August 6, 2006. http://www.ynetnews.com/articles/0,7340,L-3286880,00.html.

———. "Reuters Admits to More Image Manipulation." *Ynet*, July 8, 2006. http://www.ynetnews.com/articles/0,7340,L-3287774,00.html.

Latham, Robert, ed. *Bombs and Bandwidth: The Emerging Relationship Between Information Technology and Security*. New York: New Press, 2003.

"Lawfare in Gaza: Legislative Attack." *openDemocracy*. Accessed January 16, 2014. http://www.opendemocracy.net/article/legislative-attack.

Lawson, Sean. "The US Military's Social Media Civil War: Technology as Antagonism in Discourses of Information-Age Conflict." *Cambridge Review of International Affairs*, no. 2 (2014): 1–20.

Leibowitz, Sarah. "Lies, Folks: Hamas's Factory of False Propaganda" [in Hebrew]. *NRG*, November 27, 2012. http://www.nrg.co.il/online/1/ART2/417 /923.html.

Lemmey, Huw. "Devastation in Meatspace." *The New Inquiry*, November 28, 2012. http://thenewinquiry.com/features/devastationinmeatspace/.

Levanon, Assaf. "A Soldier 'Modeled' Next to Handcuffed Palestinian Detainees" [in Hebrew]. *Walla! News*, August 10, 2010. http://news.walla.co.il /?w=/1/1722486.

Levinson, Chaim, and Tomer Zarchin. "Netanyahu-Appointed Panel: Israel Isn't an Occupying Force in West Bank." *Haaretz.com*, July 9, 2012. http://www .haaretz.com/news/diplomacy-defense/netanyahu-appointed-panel-israel-isn -t-an-occupying-force-in-west-bank-1.449895.

Levy, Gideon. "Israel Does Not Want Peace—Israel Conference on Peace." *Haaretz.com*. Accessed July 5, 2014. http://www.haaretz.com/news/diplomacy -defense/israel-peace-conference/1.601112.

Lievouw, Leah A. "Theorizing New Media: A Meta-Theoretical Approach." *MedienJournal*, no. 3 (2002): 4–13.

Livni, Rami. "Israel's Lot After the Gaza War: Despair Without Catharsis."

Haaretz.com, August 19, 2014. http://www.haaretz.com/opinion/.premium-1 .610987.

Lomsky-Feder, Edna, and Eyal Ben-Ari. *The Military and Militarism in Israeli Society*. Albany, N.Y.: SUNY Press, 1999.

Lynch, Marc, Deen Freelon, and Sean Aday. "Syria's Socially Mediated Civil War." United States Institute of Peace, 2014.

Mackey, Robert. "Israel's Military Begins Social Media Offensive as Bombs Fall on Gaza." *The New York Times*, November 14, 2012. http://thelede.blogs.ny times.com/2012/11/14/israels-military-launches-social-media-offensive-as -bombs-fall-on-gaza/?ref=middleeast&_r=0.

———. "Israeli Ex-Soldier Defends Her Facebook Snapshots." *The New York Times*, August 17, 2010. http://thelede.blogs.nytimes.com/2010/08/17/israeli -ex-soldier-defends-her-facebook-snapshots/?_r=0.

———. "Complete Video of Israeli Raid Still Missing." *The Lede*, June 2, 2010. http://thelede.blogs.nytimes.com/2010/06/02/complete-video-of-israeli -raid-still-missing.

Magnezi, Aviel. "Was Al-Dura Video Fabricated?" *Ynet*, February 19, 2012. http://www.ynetnews.com/articles/0,7340,L-4191436,00.html.

Malkowski, Jennifer. "Streaming Death: The Politics of Dying on YouTube." *Jump Cut: A Review of Contemporary Media*, 2012. http://www.ejumpcut.org/ currentissue/malkowskiYoutubeDeaths/.

Maman, Daniel, and Eyal Ben-Ari. *Military, State, and Society in Israel: Theoretical & Comparative Perspectives*. New Brunswick, N.J.: Transaction, 2001.

Manekin, Charles. "What Youtube Finds Offensive." *The Magnes Zionist*, June 19, 2009. http://www.jeremiahhaber.com/2009/06/what-youtube-finds-offen sive.html.

Maputo, Avichai. "After the Attack: Watch the Fake Photos of Horror on the Internet" [in Hebrew]. *Feeder*. Accessed August 20, 2013. http://www .feeder.co.il/article-idf-blog-reveals-the-truth-behind-the-latest-attack-in -gaza-1000732355.

Margalit, Michal, and Yoav Zitun. "Suspended Nahal Soldier Finds Online Support for His Reinstatement." *Ynet*, April 30, 2014. http://www.ynetnews.com /articles/0,7340,L-4515034,00.html.

Marmura, Stephen M. E. *Hegemony in the Digital Age: The Arab/Israeli Conflict Online*. Lanham, MD: Lexington, 2008.

Masco, Joseph. *The Theater of Operations: National Security Affect from the Cold War to the War on Terror*. Durham, N.C.: Duke University Press, 2014.

———. "'Sensitive but Unclassified': Secrecy and the Counterterrorist State." *Public Culture* 22, no. 3 (September 21, 2010): 433–63.

Mashable. "The Israel-Gaza Conflict on Twitter." *Storify*, November 20, 2012. http://storify.com/mashable/the-israel-gaza-conflict-on-twitter.

Matar, Haggai. "Bit by Bit, Coverage of Occupation Disappears from Israeli News." *+972 Magazine*. Accessed June 25, 2014. http://972mag.com/bit-by-bit -coverage-of-occupation-disappears-from-israeli-news/33397/.

"Mates [Heb. *Sachim*]: Their Time in the Army Was the Best in Their Lives" [in Hebrew]. *Tumblr*. Accessed July 30, 2014. http://sachim.tumblr.com/post /961910853.

Mayer-Schönberger, Viktor. *Delete: The Virtue of Forgetting in the Digital Age*. Princeton, N.J.: Princeton University Press, 2011.

Mazumdar, B. Theo. "Shifting Blame on the High Seas . . . and on YouTube: The Narrative Failure of Israel's Flotilla Cyber-Diplomacy." *Global Media Journal* 12 (Fall 2012): 1–18.

McBain, Sophie. "In Syria, the Internet Has Become Just Another Battle-ground." *New Statesman*. Accessed May 27, 2014. http://www.newstatesman .com/politics/2014/04/syria-internet-has-become-just-another-battleground.

McChesney, Robert Waterman. *Digital Disconnect: How Capitalism Is Turning the Internet Against Democracy*. New York: New Press, 2013.

"The Media's Coverage of the Conflict in the North." *Honest Reporting*, August 22, 2006. http://honestreporting.com. The page is no longer available.

Mehmood, Rabia. "'Israel Is Addicted to Occupation'—Gideon Levy." *The News on Sunday*, July 27, 2014. http://tns.thenews.com.pk/israel-addicted-palestin ian-occupation/.

Mikdashi, Maya. "Can Palestinian Men Be Victims? Gendering Israel's War on Gaza." *Jadaliyya*, July 23, 2014. http://www.jadaliyya.com/pages/index/18644/ can-palestinian-men-be-victims-gendering-israels-w.

"Military Announces New Social Media Policy." *At War Blog*. Accessed May 27, 2014. http://atwar.blogs.nytimes.com/2010/02/26/military-announces-new -social-media-policy/.

Miller, D. A. "Secret Subjects, Open Secrets." *Dickens Studies Annual* 14 (1985): 17–38.

"Minister Edelstein: Goldstone Report Anti-Semitic." *Ynet*, January 1, 2010. http://www.ynetnews.com/articles/0,7340,L-3839044,00.html.

"Miraculous Recovery by Injured Gaza Man?" *Little Green Footballs*, November 15, 2012. http://littlegreenfootballs.com/page/289394_Miraculous_Recovery _by_Injured.

Mirzoeff, Nicholas. *Watching Babylon: The War in Iraq and Global Visual Culture*. New York; London: Routledge, 2004.

Mitchell, William J. *The Reconfigured Eye: Visual Truth in the Post-Photographic Era.* 1st MIT Press paperback ed. Cambridge, Mass.: MIT Press, 1994.

Mitra, Ananda. "Virtual Commonality: Looking for India on the Internet." In *Virtual Culture: Identity and Communication in Cybersociety,* ed. Steven G. Jones, 55–79. London; Thousand Oaks, Calif.: Sage, 1997.

Mizroch, Amir. "How Free Explains Israel's Flotilla FAIL." *Wired,* June 6, 2010. http://www.wired.com/2010/06/how-free-explains-israels-flotilla-fiasco.

Monterescu, Daniel, and Noa Shaindlinger. "Situational Radicalism: The Israeli 'Arab Spring' and the (Un)Making of the Rebel City." *Constellations* 20, no. 2 (2013): 229–53.

Mor, Gal. "The First Photoshop War." *Ynet,* August 17, 2006. http://www.ynet news.com/articles/0,7340,L-3292509,00.html.

Morozov, Evgeny. *The Net Delusion: How Not to Liberate the World.* London: Allen Lane, 2011.

Morris, Errol. *Believing Is Seeing: Observations on the Mysteries of Photography.* New York: Penguin Press, 2011.

Morris, GS Don. "Ruthie Blum Interviews Richard Landes." *Doc's Talk,* March 31, 2008. http://docstalk.blogspot.com/2008/03/ruthie-blum-interviews-rich ard-landes.html.

"Mowing the Lawn." *Ynet.* Accessed December 18, 2013. http://www.ynetnews .com/articles/0,7340,L-4312017,00.html.

Musleh, Maath. "Maath Musleh on Social Media and Palestine." *Jadaliyya,* January 24, 2013. http://www.jadaliyya.com/pages/index/9708/maath-musleh-on -social-media-and-palestine.

"My Life Was Threatened Because of the Photos" [in Hebrew]. *Mako,* August 17, 2010. http://www.mako.co.il/news-military/security/Article-8e1a2759fac7a21 004.htm.

Nahmias, Roee. "Arab World 'Disgusted' by IDF Facebook Photos." *Ynet,* August 17, 2010. http://www.ynetnews.com/articles/0,7340,L-3938504,00.html.

Nelson, Sarah. "World Press Photo of the Year 2013, Paul Hansen Denies Claims 'Gaza Burial' Was Faked with Photoshop." *Huffington Post,* May 14, 2013. http://www.huffingtonpost.co.uk/2013/05/14/world-press-photo-of-the -year-2013-paul-hansen-denies-claims-gaza-burial-faked-photoshop-pictures _n_3271504.html.

Neuer, Hillel. "Hamas Says Gaza 'Not Occupied'; UN Disagrees." *The Jerusalem Post,* April 4, 2012. http://www.spot.im/embed/jpostopinion.

New Profile: The Movement to Demilitarize Israeli Society. Website accessed June 25, 2014. http://www.newprofile.org/english.

Notopoulos, Katie. "Surreal Instagrams from Israel Defense Forces Soldiers."

BuzzFeed, June 4, 2012. http://www.buzzfeed.com/katienotopoulos/israeli
-soldiers-wont-let-a-little-thing-like-war.

Ochs, Juliana. *Security and Suspicion: An Ethnography of Everyday Life in Israel.*
Princeton, N.J.: Princeton University Press, 2010.

O'Neil, Lauren. "Israeli Soldiers Shock the Web with Smiling Instagram Photos."
CBC News, November 16, 2012. http://www.cbc.ca/newsblogs/yourcommu
nity/2012/11/israeli-soldiers-shock-the-web-with-smiling-instagrams.html.

"Op-Ed: The West Bank Is Under Military Occupation, and That's a Fact." *Jewish
Telegraphic Agency*, April 8, 2014. http://www.jta.org/2014/04/08/news-opin
ion/opinion/op-ed-the-west-bank-is-under-military-occupation-and-thats
-a-fact.

"Operation Pillar of Defense: Hamas Distorts Photos and Videos, the BBC Is
Misled, and the Picture Translated by Shai Atik Goes Viral on Facebook" [in
Hebrew]. *Mizbala*, November 16, 2012. http://mizbala.com/?p=57377.

Orgad, Shani. "Watching How Others Watch Us: The Israeli Media's Treatment
of International Coverage of the Gaza War." *The Communication Review* 12,
no. 3 (2009): 250–61.

*Palestinian Central Bureau of Statistics (PCBS) Reviews the Current Use of Technol-
ogy in the Palestinian Territory on the Occasion of World Information Society
Day.* Palestinian Central Bureau of Statistics, May 17, 2012.

*Palestinian ICT Sector 2.0: Technology Sector Development Report and Recommen-
dations Relevant to Regional and Global Market Opportunities.* Solutions for
Development Consulting Co., April 2013.

Peled, Ariel. "The First Social Media War Between Israel and Gaza." *The Guardian*, December 6, 2012. http://www.theguardian.com/media-network/media
-network-blog/2012/dec/06/first-social-media-war-israel-gaza.

Pereg, Noa. "Scandalous Pictures: An IDF Soldier Takes Pictures with Palestinian Detainees" [in Hebrew] *Globes*, August 16, 2010. http://www.globes.co.il/
news/article.aspx?did=1000582092&Fromelement=MoreNews.

Peri, Smadar. "IDF Hacks Nasrallah's TV Channel." *Ynet*, May 22, 2011. http://
web.archive.org/web/20110522101709/http://www.ynetnews.com/articles
/0,7340,L-3283866,00.html.

Pfeffer, Anshel. "Web Abuzz Over Soldier's Photos with Bound, Blindfolded
Inmates." *Haaretz.com*, August 17, 2010. http://www.haaretz.com/print-edition
/news/web-abuzz-over-soldier-s-photos-with-bound-blindfolded-inmates
-1.308458.

Piela, A. "I Am Just Doing My Bit to Promote Modesty: Niqabis' Self-Portraits
on Photo-Sharing Websites." *Feminist Media Studies*, no. 13 (2013): 781–90.

"PM Netanyahu's Keynote Speech at CyberTech 2014 Conference, 2014." http://www.youtube.com/watch?v=FcJawnKzi3s&feature=youtube_gdata_player.

Pötzsch, Holger. "The Emergence of iWar: Changing Practices and Perceptions of Military Engagement in a Digital Era." *New Media & Society*, December 16, 2013.

Precisely Wrong: Gaza Civilians Killed by Israeli Drone-Launched Missiles. Human Rights Watch, 2009. http://www.hrw.org/reports/2009/06/30/precisely-wrong-0.

Probyn, Elspeth. *Carnal Appetites: Foodsexidentities*. London; New York: Routledge, 2000.

"Profile: Gaza2009" [in Russian]. *LiveJournal*. Accessed August 10, 2013. http://gaza2009.livejournal.com/profile.

"Profile: Nasha_pravda_il" [in Russian]. *LiveJournal*. Accessed August 10, 2013. http://nasha-pravda -il.livejournal.com/profile.

"Protective Edge: The War of Reports on Facebook" [in Hebrew]. *Ynet*, July 24, 2014. http://www.ynet.co.il/articles/0,7340,L-4549145,00.html.

"Publication of the Government Review Committee Report Regarding Al-Durrah on France Channel 2" [in Hebrew]. The Prime Minister's Office, May 19, 2013. http://www.pmo.gov.il/English/MediaCenter/Spokesman/Pages/spokeadora190513.aspx.

Rayner, Steve. "The Novelty Trap: Why Does Institutional Learning About New Technologies Seem So Difficult?" *Industry and Higher Education* 18, no. 6 (December 1, 2004): 349–55.

Reider, Dimi. "Eden Abergil Gets Meme Treatment; Says Would Be Glad to Massacre Arabs." Dimi Reider, August 19, 2010. http://reider.wordpress.com/2010/08/19/eden-abergil-gets-meme-treatment-says-would-be-glad-to-massacre-arabs/.

———. "The Best Years of Her Life: Fond Memories of Blindfolded Prisoners." Dimi Reider, August 16, 2010. http://reider.wordpress.com/2010/08/16/the-best-years-of-her-life-fond-memories-of-blindfolded-prisoners.

———. "IDF Officer Poses with Blindfolded Palestinians, Posts Pics on Facebook." *+972 Magazine*, August 16, 2010. http://972mag.com/idf-officer-posts-images-of-blindfolded-palestinians-on-facebook-it-was-the-best-time-of-my-life/899/.

———. "Much More Graphic IDF 'Souvenir' Pictures Emerge." Dimi Reider, August 2010. http://reider.wordpress.com/2010/08/page/2/.

Remez, Didi. "Caroline Glick's 'We Con the World' and the Tea Partying of the US-Israel Relationship." *Coternet*, June 6, 2010. http://coteret.com/2010/06/06/caroline-glicks-we-con-the-world-and-the-tea-partying-of-the-us-israel-relationship/.

"The Response to the Facebook Photos: 'The IDF is an Ethical Army'" [in Hebrew]. *Walla! News*, August 18, 2010. http://news.walla.co.il/?w=/551/1723292.

Rettberg, Jill Walker. "Freshly Generated for You, and Barack Obama: How Social Media Represent Your Life." *European Journal of Communication* 24, no. 4 (2009): 451–66.

"Rock the Casba—IDF Soldiers Dancing in Hebron, July 5, 2010." http://www.youtube.com/watch?v=yqjsFExPOnM&feature=youtube_gdata_player.

"The Role of Social Media in the Syrian Civil War." MediaMeasurement. Accessed May 27, 2014. http://www.mediameasurement.com/the-role-of-social-media-in-the-syrian-civil-war/.

Ronen, Gil. "IDF's Cyber-Commander Prepares Internet Assault." *Arutz Sheva*, June 28, 2011. http://www.israelnationalnews.com/News/News.aspx/145247.

Rostovtseva, Nataliya. "Inter-Media Agenda Setting Role of the Blogosphere: A Content Analysis of the Reuters Photo Controversy Coverage During the Israel-Lebanon Conflict in 2006." Dissertation, University of North Carolina at Chapel Hill, 2009.

Russell, Jon. "Israelis Are Now the World's Biggest Social Network Addicts, Says New Report." *The Next Web*, December 22, 2011. http://thenextweb.com/socialmedia/2011/12/22/israelis-are-now-the-worlds-biggest-social-network-addicts-says-new-report/.

"Russian Jews." Facebook. Accessed August 10, 2013. https://www.facebook.com/photo.php?fbid=10151322848511955&set=a.10150241538281955.362322.1060280 21954&type=1&relevant_count=1.

Saad, Sabrine, Stéphane Bazan, and Christophe Varin. "Asymmetric Cyber-Warfare Between Israel and Hezbollah: The Web as a New Strategic Battlefield." In *Proceedings of the ACM WebSci'11*, June 14–17 2011, Klobenz, Germany, 1–4.

Sadan, Nitzan. "IDF's Facebook Dilemma." *Ynet*, August 17, 2010. http://www.ynetnews.com/articles/0,7340,L-3938318,00.html.

Samson, Elizabeth. "Is Gaza Occupied? Redefining the Legal Status of Gaza." *Mideast Security and Policy Studies*, no. 83 (2010).

Sasson-Levy, Orna. "From the Military as a Gendered Organization to Militarized Inequality Regimes: Research on Gender and the Military in Israel." *Israel Studies Review* 26, no. 2 (2011): 73–98.

———. "Individual Bodies, Collective State Interests: The Case of Israeli Combat Soldiers." *Men and Masculinities* 10, no. 3 (April 1, 2008): 296–321.

———. *Identities in Uniform: Masculinities and Femininities in the Israeli Military*. Jerusalem: Magnes Press, 2006.

———. "Gender Performance in a Changing Military: Women Soldiers in

'Masculine' Roles." *Israel Studies Forum: An Interdisciplinary Journal* 17, no. 1 (2001): 7–23.

Saunders, Robert. "Happy Slapping: Transatlantic Contagion or Home-Grown, Mass-Mediated Nihilism?" *Static*, no. 1 (2005).

"Scandal: 'Big Brother' Contestant Photographed with Bound Palestinians" [in Hebrew]. *Walla!News*, July 7, 2013. http://celebs.walla.co.il/?w=/3600/2658214.

Schechter, Asher. "Selfies in the Service of Hate," *Haaretz.com.* Accessed September 29, 2014. http://www.haaretz.com/news/features/.premium-1.602767.

———. "Liberal Zionism: It Can't Be Dead Because It Never Existed." *Haaretz. com*, August 29, 2014. http://www.haaretz.com/jewish-world/jewish-world -features/.premium-1.613037.

———. "The Social Intifada: How Millennials and Facebook Beat the Almighty Israeli Army." *Haaretz.com.* Accessed May 6, 2014. http://www.haaretz.com/ news/features/.premium-1.589032.

Schejter, Amit M., and Akiba A. Cohen. "Mobile Phone Usage as an Indicator of Solidarity: Israelis at War in 2006 and 2009." *Mobile Media & Communication* 1, no. 2 (May 1, 2013): 174–95.

Schejter, Amit M., and Noam Tirosh. "Social Media New and Old in the Al-'Arakeeb Conflict: A Case Study." *The Information Society* 28, no. 5 (2012): 304–15.

Schwartz, John. "Hacker Defaces Pro-Israel Web Site as the Mideast Conflict Expands into Cyberspace." *The New York Times*, November 3, 2000, sec. World. http://www.nytimes.com/2000/11/03/world/hacker-defaces-pro-israel-web -site-mideast-conflict-expands-into-cyberspace.html.

"The Second Draft." The Second Draft. Accessed August 16, 2013. http://www .seconddraft.org/history_pallywood.php.

Sedgwick, Eve Kosofsky. *Epistemology of the Closet.* Berkeley: University of California Press, 1990.

"Selfie, N." *OED Online.* Oxford University Press. Accessed August 1, 2014. http://www.oed.com/view/Entry/390063.

Senft, Theresa M. "Epistemology of the Second Selfie." In *LGBT Pre-Conference*. Seattle, Washington, 2014. http://www.terrisenft.net/wordpress/talks.

———. "Microcelebrity and the Branded Self." In *A Companion to New Media Dynamics*, 346–54. Oxford: Wiley-Blackwell, 2013.

Senor, Dan, Council on Foreign Relations, and Saul Singer. *Start-Up Nation: The Story of Israel's Economic Miracle*, 1st ed. New York: Twelve, 2009.

Shabi, Rachel. "Israeli Ex-Soldier Says Facebook Prisoner Pictures Were Souvenirs." *The Guardian*, August 17, 2010, sec. World news. http://www.theguard ian.com/world/2010/aug/17/israel-soldier-facebook-palestinian-prisoners.

Shachtman, Noah. "Israel's Accidental YouTube War." *Wired*, January 21, 2009. http://www.wired.com/dangerroom/2009/01/israels-acciden/.

Shamir, Shlomo. "'Twitter Revolutionized Israeli Diplomacy.'" *Haaretz.com*, June 17, 2009. http://www.haaretz.com/news/twitter-revolutionized-israeli -diplomacy-1.278260.

Shargal, Dvorit. "We Are All Eden Aberjil" [in Hebrew]. *Velvet Underground*, August 18, 2010. http://www.ice.co.il/article/view/244136.

"Shay Atik's Photos." Facebook. Accessed August 17, 2013. https://www.facebook .com/photo.php?fbid=10151159256063160&set=a.80758883159.78923.7886981 59&type=1&theater#_=_.

Shefer, Gavriel. *In Militarism and Israeli Society*. Bloomington: Indiana University Press, 2010.

Sheizaf, Noam. "Film Review: *Policeman*, a Study of the Israeli Alpha Male." *+972 Magazine*, June 21, 2014. http://972mag.com/film-review-policeman-a -study-of-the-israeli-alpha-male/92354/.

———. "Panel Appointed by Netanyahu Concludes: There Is No Occupation." *+972 Magazine*, July 9, 2012. http://972mag.com/judiciary-panel-appointed -by-netanyahu-concludes-there-is-no-occupation/50451.

Shielded from Scrutiny: IDF Violations in Jenin and Nablus. Amnesty International, November 4, 2002. http://www.amnesty.org/en/library/info/MDE15 /143/2002.

Shifman, Limor. "An Anatomy of a YouTube Meme." *New Media & Society* 14, no. 2 (March 1, 2012): 187–203.

Shmulik, Grossman. "IDF: Flotilla Participants Shot and Stabbed with Knives" [in Hebrew]. *Ynet*, May 31, 2010. http://www.ynet.co.il/articles /0,7340,L-389 6434,00.html.

Sienkiewicz, Matt. "Out of Control: Palestinian News Satire and Government Power in the Age of Social Media." *Popular Communication* 10 (October 2013): 106–18.

Silverstone, Roger. "What's New About New Media? Introduction." *New Media & Society* 1, no. 1 (April 1, 1999): 10–12.

"Social Media: The Weapon of Choice in the Gaza-Israel Conflict." *Middle East Eye*, August 21, 2014. http://www.middleeasteye.net/news/social-media -weapon-choice-gaza-israel-conflict-1807202428.

Sokatch, Daniel. "Not Only in Gaza." *New Israel Fund*, July 22, 2014. http:// www.nif.org/newmediatop/blog/1739-not-only-in-gaza.

"Soldiers' Dance in Hebron May Mean Trouble." *Ynet*. Accessed June 26, 2014. http://www.ynetnews.com/articles/0,7340,L-3915671,00.html.

"Soldiers' Photo Exhibit Strikes Nerve." CNN, June 26, 2004. http://edition
.cnn.com/2004/WORLD/meast/06/25/breaking.silence/.

Somfalvi, Attila. "Israeli Committee: Al-Dura Alive at End of Video." Ynet, May
20, 2013. http://www.ynetnews.com/articles/0,7340,L-4381574,00.html.

Sontag, Susan. Regarding the Pain of Others, 1st ed. New York: Farrar, Straus and
Giroux, 2003.

———. On Photography. New York: Dell, 1977.

Stahl, Roger. Militainment, Inc.: War, Media, and Popular Culture. New York:
Routledge, 2010.

"Stand With US UK's Photos." Facebook. Accessed August 17, 2013. https://
www.facebook.com/photo.php?fbid=386951301386318&set=a.1286295872184
92.33215.1092111185826999&type=1&theater.

"State Won't Prosecute Eden Abergil for Facebook Photos." The Jerusalem Post,
June 16, 2011. http://www.jpost.com/National-News/State-wont-prosecute
-Eden-Abergil-for-Facebook-photos.

Stein, Rebecca L. "Impossible Witness: Israeli Visuality, Palestinian Testimony,
and the Gaza War." Journal for Cultural Research 16, no. 2–3 (2012): 135–53.

———. "StateTube: Anthropological Reflections on Social Media and the Israeli State." Anthropological Quarterly 85, no. 3 (2012): 893–916.

———. "EXPLOSIVE Scenes from Israel's Gay Occupation." GLQ: A Journal
of Lesbian and Gay Studies 16, no. 4 (January 1, 2010): 517–36.

———. "Israeli Routes Through Nakba Landscapes: An Ethnographic Meditation." Jerusalem Quarterly 43 (2010): 6–17.

———. Itineraries in Conflict: Israelis, Palestinians, and the Political Lives of Tourism. Durham, N.C.: Duke University Press, 2008.

Stein, Yael. "Human Rights Violations During Operation Pillar of Defense, 14–21
November 2012." B'Tselem, May 2013.

Steinberg, Jessica. "The 'Matzav:' Etymology of a Word." The Jewish Federations
of North America, September 2013. http://www.jewishfederations.org/page
.aspx?id=33402.

Steiner, Peter. "On the Internet, Nobody Knows You're a Dog." The New Yorker,
July 5, 1992.

Stelter, Brian. "Videos Carry On the Fight Over Sea Raid." The New York Times,
June 1, 2010, sec. World / Middle East. http://www.nytimes.com/2010/06/02/
world/middleeast/02media.html.

Stewart, Kathleen. Ordinary Affects. Durham, N.C.: Duke University Press, 2007.

Stone, Allucquere Rosanne. "Will the Real Body Please Stand Up?: Boundary
Stories About Virtual Cultures." In Cyberspace: First Steps, ed. Michael Bene-
dikt. Cambridge, Mass.: MIT Press, 1992.

Struk, Janina. *Private Pictures: Soldiers' Inside View of War.* London; New York: I.B. Tauris, 2011.

Sucharov, Mira, and Brent E. Sasley. "Blogging Identities on Israel/Palestine: Public Intellectuals and Their Audiences." *PS: Political Science & Politics* 47, no. 1 (2014): 177–81.

Sumiala, Johanna Maaria, and Minttu Tikka. "Broadcast Yourself—Global News! A Netnography of the 'Flotilla' News on YouTube." *Communication, Culture & Critique* 6, no. 2 (June 1, 2013): 318–35.

Susca, Margot A. "Why We Still Fight: Adolescents, America's Army, and the Government-Gaming Nexus." *Global Media Journal* 12 (Spring 2012): 1–16.

Sutter, John D. "Will Twitter War Become the New Norm?" CNN, November 19, 2012. http://www.cnn.com/2012/11/15/tech/social-media/twitter-war-gaza -israel/.

Swed, Ori, and John Sibley Butler. "Military Capital in the Israeli Hi-Tech Industry." *Armed Forces & Society*, no. 1 (2015): 123–41.

"Talk of the Day: 'David Nahlawi' as a National Hero" [in Hebrew]. Reshet TV. Accessed June 26, 2014. http://reshet.tv/Shows/todays_talk/videomark list,234627.

Taussig, Michael T. *Defacement: Public Secrecy and the Labor of the Negative.* Stanford, Calif.: Stanford University Press, 1999.

Tawil-Souri, Helga. "Digital Occupation: Gaza's High-Tech Enclosure." *Journal of Palestine Studies* 41, no. 2 (January 1, 2012): 27–43.

"TinEye." Accessed February 3, 2014. http://www.tineye.com/about.

Toobin, Jeffrey. "The Solace of Oblivion." *The New Yorker*, September 29, 2014. http://www.newyorker.com/magazine/2014/09/29/solace-oblivion.

"The Truth About the Middle East." Facebook. Accessed September 22, 2014. http://www.facebook.com/photo.php?fbid=474872465898136&set=a.474033 639315352.122949.473807642671285&type=1&relevant_count=1).

"The Truth About the Middle East." Facebook. Accessed July 30, 2014. https:// www.facebook.com/TheTruthABoutTheMiddleEast?sk=info.

"The Truth About the Middle East." Facebook. Accessed November 22, 2012. https://www.facebook.com/photo.php?fbid=475015445883838&set=a.474033 639315352.122949.473807642671285&type=1&relevant_count=1.

Tsoref, Ayala. "Israel Preparing Itself for Twitter War Over Palestinian State." *Haaretz.com*, May 25, 2011. http://www.haaretz.com/business/israel-prepar ing-itself-for-twitter-war-over-palestinian-state-1.363910.

———. "3 Most Viewed YouTube Clips in the World—Posted by IDF—Israel News." *Haaretz.com*, June 3, 2010. http://www.haaretz.com/news/diplomacy -defense/3-most-viewed-youtube-clips-in-the-world-posted-by-idf-1.293994.

Tsuk, Nirit. "Online Incitement: It's Up to the Parents" [in Hebrew]. *NRG*, July 31, 2014. http://www.nrg.co.il/online/1/ART2/611/173.html.

"Underground Weapons Storage Facility in Gaza Struck by Israel Air Force, January 1, 2009." http://www.youtube.com/watch?v=hV6l4CSwL6c&feature=you tube.

Usher, Nikki B. "Reviewing Fauxtography: A Blog-Driven Challenge to Mass Media Power Without the Promises of Networked Publicity." *First Monday* 13, no. 12 (November 29, 2008). doi:10.5210/fm.v13i12.2158.

Vacca, John R. *Guide to Wireless Network Security*. New York: Springer, 2006.

"Video of Naked Soldiers Goes Viral." *Ynet*, June 11, 2013. http://www.ynetnews .com/articles/0,7340,L-4391178,00.html.

Virilio, Paul. *War and Cinema: The Logistics of Perception*. London; New York: Verso, 1989.

Vis, Farida. "Collecting Data for #pillarofdefense and #failing: On the Complexities of Real-Time Data Collection on Twitter." Presented at the Social Media and Political Horizons: Israel/Palestine: The Middle East and Beyond. The University of Manchester, United Kingdom, 2013.

Vivienne, S., and J. Burgess. "The Remediation of the Personal Photograph and the Politics of Self-Representation in Digital Storytelling." *Journal of Material Culture*, no. 3 (2013): 279–98.

Wallace-Wells, Benjamin. "Why Israel Is Losing the American Media War." *Daily Intelligencer*, July 20, 2014. http://nymag.com/daily/intelligencer/2014/07/ why-israel-is-losing-the-american-media-war.html.

Ward, Will. "Social Media in the Gaza Conflict." *Arab Media & Society*, 2009. http://www.arabmediasociety.com/articles/downloads/20090121104211_AMS7 _Will_Ward.pdf.

"Was the 'Picture of the Year' of a Children's Funeral in Gaza Fabricated?" [in Hebrew]. *Walla! News*, May 15, 2013. http://news.walla.co.il/?w=/14/2642328.

Weimann, Gabriel. *Terror on the Internet: The New Arena, the New Challenges*. United States Institute of Peace, May 2010.

Weiner, Stuart. "Netanyahu: Hamas Wants 'Telegenically Dead Palestinians.'" *Times of Israel*, July 20, 2014. http://www.timesofisrael.com/netanyahu-hamas -wants-telegenically-dead-palestinians.

Weiss, Itzik, and Maxim Lango. "An Officer in the Army Spokesman's Unit Admits: The Soldiers' Protest Is Justified" [in Hebrew]. *0404 Blog*, February 5, 2014. http://0404.co.il/post/7138.

Weitz, Gidi. "Signs of Fascism in Israel Reached New Peak During Gaza Op, Says Renowned Scholar." *Haaretz.com*, September 3, 2014. http://www.haaretz .com/news/features/.premium-1.610368.

Weizman, Eyal. *The Least of All Possible Evils?: Humanitarian Violence from Arendt to Gaza*. London?; New York: Verso, 2011.

———. *Hollow Land?: Israel's Architecture of Occupation*. London: Verso, 2007.

Wolfgang, Ernst. *Digital Memory and the Archive*. Minneapolis: University of Minnesota Press, 2012.

"The World Bank DataBank: Israel." Accessed October 3, 2013. http://databank .worldbank.org/data/views/reports/tableview.aspx#.

Yahav, Nir. "The Arab Press: 'The Soldier's Photographs Are Sadistic'" [in Hebrew]. *Walla! News*, August 18, 2010. http://news.walla.co.il/?w=/1/1723247.

Yar, Majid. "Crime, Media and the Will-to-Representation: Reconsidering Relationships in the New Media Age." *Crime, Media, Culture* 8, no. 3 (December 1, 2012): 245–60. doi:10.1177/1741659012443227.

Yaron, Oded. "IDF Soldier Posts Instagram Photo of Palestinian Boy in Crosshairs of Sniper Rifle." *Haaretz.com*, February 18, 2013. http://www.haaretz.com /news/diplomacy-defense/idf-soldier-posts-instagram-photo-of-palestinian -boy-in-crosshairs-of-sniper-rifle-1.504117.

———. "Tip: How to Recognize a Fake Photograph" [in Hebrew]. *Haaretz.com*, November 22, 2012. http://www.haaretz.co.il/captain/software/1.1871344.

Yasur-Beit Or, Meital. "No Shrapnel Found in Gaza Victim's Body." *Ynet*, June 20, 2006. http://www.ynetnews.com/articles/0,7340,L-3265297,00.html.

Yosef, Raz. *Beyond Flesh?: Queer Masculinities and Nationalism in Israeli Cinema*. New Brunswick, N.J.: Rutgers University Press, 2004.

Younge, Gary. "Blame the White Trash." *The Guardian*, May 17, 2004. http:// www.theguardian.com/world/2004/may/17/iraq.usa5.

Ziccardi, Giovanni. *Resistance, Liberation Technology and Human Rights in the Digital Age*. Dordrecht: Springer, 2013.

Zitun, Yoav. "Soldiers Disciplined for Mistreating Palestinian Detainees." *Ynet*, February 17, 2013. http://www.ynetnews.com/articles/0,7340,L-4345833,00.html.

Ziv, Amitai. "Israel's Defense Ministry Signs Deal for Military-Grade Smartphones." *Haaretz.com*, March 1, 2014. http://www.haaretz.com/news/diplo macy-defense/.premium-1.566862.

Zonszein, Mairav. "PHOTO: Soldier Punches Palestinian Activist in the Face." *+972 Magazine*. Accessed June 26, 2014. http://972mag.com/photo-soldier -punches-palestinian-activist-in-the-face/91813/.

———. "WATCH: IDF Does Not Want You to See What Occupation Looks Like." *+972 Magazine*, March 24, 2013. http://972mag.com/watch-idf-does -not-want-you-to-see-what-occupation-looks-like/68129/.

Zuckerman, Ethan. "Understanding #amina." *My Heart's in Accra*, June 13, 2011. http://www.ethanzuckerman.com/blog/2011/06/13/understanding-amina /#comments.

Index

Stanford Studies in Middle Eastern and Islamic Societies and Cultures

---

Bassam Haddad, *Business Networks in Syria: The Political Economy of Authoritarian Resilience*
2011

Noah Coburn, *Bazaar Politics: Power and Pottery in an Afghan Market Town*
2011

Laura Bier, *Revolutionary Womanhood: Feminisms, Modernity, and the State in Nasser's Egypt*
2011

Samer Soliman, *The Autumn of Dictatorship: Fiscal Crisis and Political Change in Egypt under Mubarak*
2011

Rochelle A. Davis, *Palestinian Village Histories: Geographies of the Displaced*
2010

Haggai Ram, *Iranophobia: The Logic of an Israeli Obsession*
2009

John Chalcraft, *The Invisible Cage: Syrian Migrant Workers in Lebanon*
2008

Rhoda Kanaaneh, *Surrounded: Palestinian Soldiers in the Israeli Military*
2008

Asef Bayat, *Making Islam Democratic: Social Movements and the Post-Islamist Turn*
2007

Robert Vitalis, *America's Kingdom: Mythmaking on the Saudi Oil Frontier*
2006

Jessica Winegar, *Creative Reckonings: The Politics of Art and Culture in Contemporary Egypt*
2006

Joel Beinin and Rebecca L. Stein, editors, *The Struggle for Sovereignty: Palestine and Israel, 1993–2005*
2006